Esteemed Reproach

BAPTISTS
HISTORY, LITERATURE, THEOLOGY, HYMNS

General Editor: Walter B. Shurden is the Callaway Professor of Christianity in the Roberts Department of Christianity and Executive Director of the Center for Baptist Studies, Mercer University, Macon, Georgia.

John Taylor, *Baptists on the American Frontier: A History of Ten Baptist Churches*
   Edited by Chester Young
Thomas Helwys, *A Short Declaration of the Mystery of Iniquity*
   Edited by Richard Groves
Roger Williams, *The Bloody Tenant of Persecution for Cause of Conscience*
   Edited by Richard Groves; Edwin Gaustad, Historical Introduction
James A. Rogers†, *Richard Furman: Life and Legacy*
Lottie Moon, *Send the Light: Lottie Moon's Letters and Other Writings*
   Edited by Keith Harper
James Byrd, *The Challenges of Roger Williams: Religious Liberty, Violent Persecution, and the Bible*
Anne Dutton, *The Influential Spiritual Writings of Anne Dutton: Volume 1: Letters*
   Edited by JoAnn Ford Watson (Fall 2003)
David T. Morgan, *Southern Baptist Sisters: In Search of Status, 1845-2000*
   (Fall 2003)
William E. Ellis, *"A Man of Books and a Man of the People"*:
   E. Y. Mullins and the Crisis of Moderate Southern Baptist Leadership
   (paperback Fall 2003; hardback 1985)
Jarrett Burch, *Adiel Sherwood: Baptist Antebellum Pioneer in Georgia* (Winter 2003)
Anthony Chute, *A Piety Above the Common Standard: Jesse Mercer and the Defense of Evangelistic Calvinism* (Spring 2004)
Annie Armstrong, *Rescue the Perishing: Selected Correspondence of Annie W. Armstrong*
   Edited by Keith Harper (Spring 2004)
William H. Brackney, *A Genetic History of Baptist Thought* (Fall 2004)
Henlee Hulix Barnette, *A Pilgrimage of Faith: My Story* (Fall 2004)
Anne Dutton, *The Influential Spiritual Writings of Anne Dutton: Volume 2: Discourses, Poetry, Hymns, Memoir*
   Edited by JoAnn Ford Watson (Fall 2004)
Walter B. Shurden, *Not an Easy Journey: Some Transitions in Baptist Life* (Spring 2005)
Marc A. Jolley, editor, *Distinctively Baptist: Essays on Baptist History: Festschrift Walter B. Shurden* (Spring 2005)

Esteemed Reproach

The Lives of Rev. James Ireland

and Rev. Joseph Craig

Edited by

Keith Harper and C. Martin Jacumin

MERCER UNIVERSITY PRESS

MACON, GEORGIA

25TH ANNIVERSARY

ISBN 0-86554-914-1
MUP/P270

The paper used in this publication meets the minimum
requirements of American National Standard for Information
Sciences—Permanence of Paper for Printed Library Materials,
ANSI Z39.48-1992.

Library of Congress Cataloging-in-Publication Data

Esteemed reproach : the lives of Rev. James Ireland and Rev.
Joseph Craig / edited by Keith Harper and Martin Jacumin.—
1st ed. p. cm.
Includes bibliographical references (p.   ) and index.
ISBN 0-86554-914-1 (pbk. : alk. paper)
1. Ireland, James, 1748-1806. 2. Craig, Joseph, Rev.
3. Baptists—Clergy—Biography. 4. Baptists—History.
5. Virginia—Church history.
I. Harper, Keith, 1957- II. Jacumin, Martin, 1966- III. Ireland,
James, 1748-1806. Life of the Rev. James Ireland. IV. Craig,
Joseph, Rev. History of Rev. Joseph Craig.
BX6493.E88 2005
286'.1'0922755--dc22

2005002557

Contents

For

Mary Lou Stephens

Whose faithful, conscientious service

Has been a blessing to many

"… for her price is above rubies"
Proverbs 31:10

Preface

It has been our distinct pleasure to edit *Esteemed Reproach: The Lives of Rev. James Ireland and Rev. Joseph Craig*. Before proceeding, however, we would like to clarify some of our editorial decisions.

Editing someone else's writing is never easy, especially when the works in question are nearly 200 years old. We had two separate texts, *The Life of the Rev. James Ireland* and *The History of Rev. Joseph Craig* that we edited into this one volume, each posing its own editorial challenges. For example, just before he died in 1806 James Ireland recounted his life's story to a second party. His scribe apparently finished a manuscript and delivered it to a printer, but never completed the publication process. Several years passed before a third party located the printed, albeit incomplete work. This unnamed third party added a few of his own observations to the text that he found and published *The Life of the Rev. James Ireland* in 1819. Joseph Craig's autobiography is also somewhat curious. In 1927, a certain Aubrey Thomas published *The History of Rev. Joseph Craig*. The book claimed to be based on Craig's "journal" and, most likely, Thomas used the original work to produce this limited edition booklet for Craig's descendants. Unfortunately, we found no trace of Craig's original journal and therefore could not clarify certain awkward portions of Thomas's narrative. For instance, Thomas's text sometimes uses dashes for no apparent reason and we guessed that he may have been indicating portions of Craig's work that were either illegible or missing words. Thomas's text also contains some material that we chose not to include because it had no direct bearing on Joseph Craig.

In addition to their age and obscure origins, both works posed grammatical and stylistic challenges. When we encountered variant spellings for words within the texts we chose to use the most common modern spelling for uniformity's sake. Thus, "burthen" became burden, "enquire" became inquire, and so forth. We also chose to retain British spellings.

Capitalization proved to be a real adventure because neither of our works capitalized words in a uniform style. We therefore chose to capitalize divine pronouns like He, Him, Thee, and Thou, as well as all divine references, but we chose not to capitalize adjectives that modified divine references unless it was a commonly accepted biblical reference like "Great Shepherd." We chose to capitalize Satan as a proper name, but we did not capitalize "scripture" and "gospel." We made minimal alterations to the original texts but on those rare occasions when we questioned original usage we used [?] to indicate what we thought might be a better word choice, as in Book 3, Chapter 9 of Ireland's work where the compiler mistakenly refers to Philemon's servant as Theophilus, rather than Onesimus. Finally, we thought that it might be helpful if we divided certain portions of text into shorter paragraphs, especially when some paragraphs were three pages long. We hope our modifications are clear and helpful.

Having offered our grammatical and stylistic caveats, we now turn to a more pleasant pursuit, namely offering our sincere thanks to those who helped us bring this project to life. First, we owe Lynne Hollingsworth and the Kentucky Historical Society a tremendous debt of gratitude. Lynne provided us with *two* usable copies of *The History of Rev. Joseph Craig* and the Society graciously allowed us to reprint it. We thank them both. We also thank Dr. Shawn Madden, Senior Librarian at Southeastern Baptist Theological Seminary, Wake Forest, NC, and Bill Sumners, Director and Archivist for the Southern Baptist Historical Library and Archives, Nashville, TN, for their timely assistance with much-needed documents. We also thank Jim Lutzweiler, Poet Laureate of Schnappsburg, part-time, of course, and Archivist for Southeastern Baptist Theological Seminary who freely offered his advice even though we consistently ignored it. We *did* follow Marc Jolley's advice and working with the staff at Mercer University Press was a joy—as always. We also listened to Michael Travers and David Beck whose sound advice on grammar and style greatly improved our work. On a personal note, our families were supportive throughout this project and we commend Lori Jacumin and Johnnie Harper, as well as Morgan, Jarrett, and Sarah Beth Jacumin, and David Harper for their love and good-natured encouragement.

Finally, we offer our sincere thanks to Melissa Latham and Mary Lou Stephens for typing this work's first draft, helping to proofread it, and then typing the seemingly endless wave of corrections that followed each proofreading session. They are both delighted that this project is completed and we could not have done it without them. Mary Lou, however, is excited for another reason. In December 2003, she finished her 25th year of service at Southeastern Baptist Theological Seminary and then headed straight to the beach in retirement. She has taken pride in her work, served her professors with distinction, and we will all miss her. Mary Lou, we dedicate this book to you as a small token of appreciation for all you have done to make Southeastern the great institution that it is.

Keith Harper
C. Martin Jacumin
Wake Forest, North Carolina
September 2004

Introduction

On Tuesday, June 17, 1806, the *Winchester Virginia Gazette* published an obituary for Elder James Ireland, one of Virginia's best-known Baptist ministers. He was only fifty-eight years old when he died, but his ministry had lasted nearly forty years. Ireland was an energetic minister – he served three churches as pastor in two different counties, despite the fact that he had numerous physical infirmities. "He was always distinguished as an able minister of the New Testament," the *Gazette* observed, "rightly dividing the word of truth, giving to saint and sinner their portion in due season." His final days found him tranquil, fully prepared to leave this world with confidence that he would be received into heaven's rest.[1]

Those who had known "little Jamie Ireland" as a youth would scarcely recognize their old playmate from his obituary. The Ireland they knew enjoyed singing, dancing, and bawdy humor. By his own admission, Ireland came to America after committing an unspecified "indiscretion" that compelled him to seek a safer home. Obviously, something happened to this young rascal that dramatically changed his life.

James Ireland was born in Edinburgh, Scotland, in 1748 where his mother and father reared him in a strong Presbyterian household. The Irelands were fairly well to do, and they lived comfortably. His father provided the best possible education for young James who proved to be a

---

[1] For the brief but rather complicated history of the *Winchester Virginia Gazette* see Clarence S. Brigham's *History and Bibliography of American Newspapers, 1690-1820* (Worcester, MA: American Antiquarian Society, 1947) 1166-1167. Of eleven collections who have this paper none has a complete run and none has the June 17, 1806 edition. See p. 160 for the text of Ireland's obituary as it appeared in the 1819 edition of *The Life of the Rev. James Ireland*.

good student, as well as a "class clown." At some point, he decided that he no longer wished to study, but rather wanted to live an adventurous life at sea. His father arranged for James to make several voyages, some of which placed him in considerable danger. In his more mature reflections, Ireland claimed that God's providential hand had spared him through many nautical perils. As a lad, however, hurricanes and ice floes merely taught him that he was not cut out to be a sailor.

Upon coming to America, Ireland became the headmaster of a small school in Shenandoah County, Virginia. He was only about eighteen years old, but he tolerated none of the shenanigans from his students that he had labored to perfect back in Scotland. He quickly gained acceptance within his community and established a reputation for enjoying a good time. He had few religious inclinations apart from his life-long reverence for the Lord's Day and felt comfortable with almost everyone. "With the religious," he claimed, "I could moralize a little; with the well-bred I could be polite: with the merry I could be antic, and with the obscene I could be profane." He enjoyed his status as both schoolmaster and party favorite.

Ireland's conversion and subsequent abandonment of his "old way" proved to be difficult. At some point, Nicholas Fane, a local Baptist preacher, challenged him to write a poem on charity. Well satisfied with Ireland's work, Fane challenged him to produce a second poem on "the natural man's dependence for heaven." Composing this work forced Ireland to ponder his own spiritual pilgrimage. After considerable personal agony and doubt, Ireland finally found peace and spiritual fulfillment. At first, his friends reacted with varying degrees of astonishment. A couple of men swore that they would lure him back to his old friends and their old ways only to be converted themselves.

Ireland began preaching the gospel soon after his conversion. He quickly developed a reputation for both his pulpit skills and theological knowledge, but he was not sure about his religious affiliation. He had no desire to be an Anglican; neither did he want to return to his Presbyterian roots. He had heard many evil things about the Baptists and at one time had even sworn never to become one. After careful consideration, however, Ireland decided to seek baptism by immersion and ordination at a meeting of the Sandy Creek Association in North

Carolina in 1769. He chose to align himself with Separate Baptists rather than Regular Baptists because of their zeal and emotional preaching style. Unfortunately for Ireland, this particular meeting was consumed by an unusual amount of Associational business and the attendees had no time to address Ireland's concerns. Once back in Virginia, Samuel Harris, one of the region's most respected Baptist leaders, baptized Ireland who immediately launched his career as a Baptist preacher.[2]

Ireland's enthusiastic preaching soon landed him in jail. As colonial governments inched closer to the American Revolution, some Baptists, particularly those in Virginia, were coming under increasing scrutiny. Earlier in the eighteenth century they had scarcely been worth noticing, but the Great Awakening claimed numerous converts and by the mid 1760s, local courts had begun curbing perceived Baptist excesses.[3] Baptist calls for religious liberty and their denunciation of various upper-class status symbols has led one scholar to argue that evangelicals "transformed" Virginia by eroding the gentry's power base.[4] Yet, Ireland and his cohorts may not have agreed that the gentry lost much by way of power. As he languished in Culpeper jail from November 1769 to April 1770, Ireland faced privation, persecution, and several attempts on his life. His graceful response to adversity is one of the most evocative episodes in American Baptist history. Ultimately, Ireland survived his ordeal but life after his imprisonment was not always blissful. On the one hand, he labored happily doing what he enjoyed most, namely church work. He enjoyed great success as pastor of Buck's Marsh, Water Lick, and Happy Creek churches.[5] On the other hand,

---

[2] See Robert Baylor Semple, *History of the Baptists in Virginia*, revised and extended by G. W. Beale (Lafayette, TN: Church History Research and Archives, 1976, reprinted from 1894 revised edition) 383. Semple also notes that at some point Ireland switched affiliation from Separate Baptist to Regular Baptist, thereby avoiding a certain amount of persecution.

[3] Ibid., 10-92. See Appendix for a summary of how Baptists were persecuted in Virginia.

[4] See Rhys Isaac, *The Transformation of Virginia, 1740-1790* (New York & London: W. W. Norton & Company, 1982).

[5] Buck's Marsh also appears in other sources as Buck Marsh and Buckmarsh. We used "Buck's Marsh" in this work primarily because Ireland's obituary says

Ireland occasionally faced physical intimidation and harassment wherever he preached. Moreover, Ireland's family servant, Sucky, and a houseguest poisoned him and his family in 1792. His would-be assassins were tried and acquitted, despite the fact that Ireland's son William ingested a lethal dose of poison. Ireland recovered but his mistreatment while imprisoned in Culpeper jail along with his subsequent hardships probably shortened his life significantly.

In contrast to James Ireland's steady, faithful ministry, Joseph Craig was mercurial and unpredictable. Craig and his brothers, Lewis and Elijah, frequently ran afoul of the law for preaching the gospel. Their boldness earned them persecution and regular appearances before Old Dominion magistrates. In 1781, they along with their kin and numerous friends formed a group that has since earned the nickname, "The Traveling Church," and relocated to Kentucky. A feisty little man, "stoop shouldered" with a "hardy complexion," Joseph Craig possessed none of the organizational and administrative gifts of his better-known brothers. His own testimony suggests that he frequently spent weeks away from home on various preaching engagements. He made at least one attempt at pastoral ministry when he established the Head of Boone's Creek Church in 1785. He served this congregation until some time in 1790 when he left abruptly and the church subsequently disbanded.[6]

Craig tried to compensate for his lack of spiritual giftedness with zeal. According to Kentucky Baptist historian J. H. Spencer, Lewis Craig once mused that his brother might be doing God's kingdom more harm than good, seeing that he had been "trying to preach" for twenty years and only had one convert to show for his effort. Joseph Craig then

---

that he served "Baptist congregations at Buck's Marsh, Happy Creek and Water Lick, in Frederick and Shenandoah Counties Virginia."

[6] For a description of Joseph Craig see John Taylor, *A History of Ten Baptist Churches* (New York: Arno Press, 1980; reprinted from the second edition, 1827) 280-282. For the sketchy details of Craig's tenure at Head of Boone's Creek Church see J. H. Spencer, *A History of Kentucky Baptists*, revised and corrected by Burrilla B. Spencer, 2 vol. (Cincinnati: J. R. Baumes, 1885, reprinted by Church History Research and Archives, Gallatin, TN, 1984) 1:81.

thanked God and eagerly volunteered to preach twenty years more for another conversion.[7]

Craig's zeal notwithstanding, his eccentricities could be disconcerting. John Taylor, a well-known Virginia Baptist preacher who also relocated to Kentucky, held the Craig family in high regard but occasionally found himself embarrassed by Joseph's antics, beginning with their initial meeting. Taylor recalled preaching a candlelight meeting at the lower South River Church in Virginia. When the service ended Joseph Craig ran up to him and exclaimed, "Here is the ass's colt that my Master rode to Jerusalem." Craig may have meant that Taylor had done an excellent job of "conveying" Jesus to the people, but he never bothered to explain precisely what he meant. "After this," Taylor noted, "Craig would introduce me to strangers as 'the ass's colt' without telling them my name."[8] Of course, Taylor also appreciated the methods Craig devised for baffling those who tried to arrest him whether it involved running through swamps, climbing trees to avoid bloodhounds, or pretending to be completely deranged.

While Joseph Craig may not have enjoyed widespread success in Christian ministry, he worked hard and instilled his work ethic into his children. He excelled in business ventures and may well have been the most successful businessman in the entire Craig family. He amassed significant wealth in Kentucky and according to Taylor, Craig's children all enjoyed a measure of affluence, respect from their neighbors, and they were all active church members as of the 1820s.[9]

If their personal testimonies reveal their courage and conviction, their poetry offers insight into the depths of their spiritual dedication. Both Ireland and Craig expressed themselves through warm, devotional verses that appear to have flowed freely from their souls. Ireland's warning that the "natural man" is hopeless without Christ is far more than a grim reminder of Judgment Day; it offers hope in Christ. Craig's desire to serve Christ is apparent in each of his poems, as is a sense of

---

[7] Spencer, *A History of Kentucky Baptists*, 1:83.

[8] John Taylor, *Baptists on the American Frontier: A History of Ten Baptist Churches of Which the Author has Alternately Been A Member*, ed. Chester Raymond Young, annotated third edition (Macon: Mercer University Press, 1995) 105.

[9] Taylor, *A History of Ten Baptist Churches*, 282.

his disappointment that he did not have a more active role in doing Christ's bidding. Their varied subjects and audiences indicate that Ireland and Craig both saw pastoral ministry as something far more than preaching. They believed that pastors needed to "tend their flocks," a feat each attempted in his own way.

The similarities between their life stories notwithstanding, the most striking thing about these men may be their post-conversion spirituality. Ireland struggled with his sinfulness before his conversion, but if he doubted God's love or his own Christian sincerity after his conversion, he said nothing about it. As he recollected, he hoped that he might become a preacher and was overjoyed when he felt called into the ministry. On the other hand, Craig never enjoyed the same kind of security that calmed Ireland's spirit. On the contrary, Craig repeatedly noted that he felt as if God had withdrawn from him, leaving him to wonder if God really loved him. Whereas Ireland experienced a heavenly peace of mind and spirit, Craig continually seems to be on guard for the slightest hint that God approved of him and what he was doing.

On January 16, 1786 the Virginia Legislature passed the Virginia Statute for Religious Freedom. Religious dissenters celebrated the decision and praised Thomas Jefferson and James Madison for their commitment to religious liberty.[10] But, this newfound freedom came with a price, a fact that Virginia's Baptists knew only too well. Many of their number had suffered inhumane treatment and brutality at their neighbors' hands. Yet, they all bore their reproach with a certain esteem. That is, they were thankful that they had been counted worthy to suffer for Christ's sake. According to one historian some forty-five Baptist preachers were jailed for various crimes against the state church in late eighteenth century Virginia. Only two, James Ireland and Joseph Craig, left first-hand accounts of their tribulations.[11] Their moving testimonies of life without the privilege of religious toleration serve as

---

[10] For a brief discussion of religious turmoil in late Colonial/Early National Virginia, see Merrill D. Peterson, *Thomas Jefferson & the New Nation: A Biography* (New York & London: Oxford University Press, 1970) 133-144.

[11] Taylor, *Baptists on the American Frontier*, pp. 88-89, see note 23.

enduring reminders that Baptists played a significant role in securing this nation's religious liberty.

The Life of the Rev. James Ireland

Preface to

The Life Of The Rev. James Ireland

1819 Edition

The principal part of the following history was written by the author's amanuensis, while he was confined to his bed by sickness, from which he never recovered; and it was, in consequence of a pressing solicitation by James Ireland, eldest son of the deceased and the widow of the deceased, that the compiler was prevailed on to undertake the work. What was written was in quarto but very little of it paged, and the sheets were found without being arranged. There can be no doubt, from what the compiler has been told, but that the amanuensis wrote in a great hurry which made it necessary to transcribe a considerable part of the original manuscript; while doing this and revising and correcting the other part, it was conceived that it would be of some advantage to the reader to divide the work into three books, and those books into chapters.

The first book contains the history of the life of the author from his birth, in the city of Edinburgh, Scotland, until his manhood; when we find him on this side of the Atlantic, teaching school near a place then called the Cross Roads, but now it is a post town, called New Market, Shenandoah County, State of Virginia; and there, after arriving almost to the highest pitch of vanity, we find him, through the powerful and mysterious workings of grace, arrested by his God, and under deep conviction for sin.

The second book gives an account of his pungent and lengthy convictions and temptations, and his happy conversion, and deliverance from the burden of his sins, etc. The third book gives an account of his baptism, his labours in the ministry, his imprisonment by his persecutors and his release; his great success in the ministry, his marriages, sufferings and death; to which is added some poems of his own composition, and a brief account of his family, etc.

It appears by the beginning of the first chapter of the following work, that Mr. Ireland had written (either with his own hand, or by that of his amanuensis) an introduction to this work; but when the sheets containing the manuscript came to be collected (which was some years after Mr. Ireland's death) nothing of it was to be found. Had Mr. Ireland lived to have had his history, or so much of it as he intended leisurely written out by his amanuensis, no doubt but much more interesting matter would have been presented to the reader; but this was not the case; yet if God should please to grant His blessing to what is here presented to the reader, and if he be yet in his sins, and under the condemnatory sentence of God's righteous law, and this should prove a means, in the hands of the Spirit, of his conviction and conversion; or should the reader be already a believer, and this work should prove a means of his edification, comfort and establishment; then the desired end will be abundantly answered. Although many parts of this work may prove both pleasing and entertaining, merely as a history, the main design of the subject of it, was the good of immortal souls.

THE COMPILER.

THE LIFE, etc.

Chapter I

The disadvantages the Author laboured under in the present undertaking—gives an account of his ancestors, or parentage—that he was taught the externals of Presbyterianism—had a tenacious retentive memory, as well as a heart susceptible of tender feelings—believes all beggars went to heaven, and that their blessing would take others there. About this time Mr. G. Whitefield preached in Edinburgh, and though the author was but a boy then, he believed Mr. W. was instrumental in converting his father.

Having given some intimation of my intention of writing a history of my life, with the motives which have induced me to undertake the task, together with the obstructions that prevented my executing it, at an earlier period, and the urgent necessity which requires, that if wrote at all it must be done speedily, must serve as my apology for now commencing the work. And duty requires me to observe, that it is begun under a very singular disadvantage, arising from my present low state of health, and weak habit of body.

Heretofore, whenever I had occasion to write, the heart, that dictated the subject, the mind that arranged the ideas, and the hand that recorded the form, were all united with the same body; hence, the component parts were more easily united and drawn in connection with the whole; and the symmetry of the whole more apparent. But the case is now different with me, I am confined to bed with a languishing sickness, and am wholly dependent, for the mechanical part of the work, on the helping hand of a friend; who like Baruch the son of Neriah has to write all the words from my mouth. This circumstance will, I doubt not, render the relation more incorrect, and the chain of events less connected than they might otherwise have been; but the great object I have in view is, to give a just relation of the wonderful dealings of a gracious God to me a sinner; and if it is destitute of the embellishment of learning or grammatical precision, it is of but little moment to me, so that it finds acceptance among the humble followers of the dear Redeemer, for whose comfort and encouragement in their heavenly pilgrimage, the work is undertaken, and to whom, it is respectfully dedicated.

It is customary, when the history of a person's life is published, to give an account of the place of his nativity and parentage. The object I have in view, in this particular is only, so far as is necessary, to introduce me as a rational being in the world.

My ancestors in the male line, were a respectable people, and were neither classed with the nobility nor commonalty, but occupied the middle space between these appellations, and were ranked with those who according to the custom of the country, were denominated gentry: and on the maternal side I sprang from a people that were called good farmers. My grandfather's name was Thomas Andrews. My grandfather in the male lineage lived in a town eight miles from Edinburgh, called Kings-horn, being a small seaport, and had his landed estate lying contiguous thereto; he was bred to the profession of the law, and was considered as an able counselor; and enjoyed other offices that were profitable and advantageous. He had three sons named George, David and James.

All my connections on that side, as far as I knew them, had generally some post in the military or sea service, or else were bred to the law. My eldest uncle George embraced a military life, which so exasperated his father that he disinherited him, as I have heard my parents say, and left his landed estate to his second son David, except a few improvements in the town that were left for his oldest grandchildren. My father, the youngest of his sons, on whom he bestowed a very liberal education, was bred to the law; whether the commencement of his studies in that profession were under his own father I cannot ascertain, but have heard him say, he finished his studies in Edinburgh; where, in process of time, he married my mother and fixed his residence in that city.

Their offspring consisted of seven children, of whom I was second in age; my elder brother George, when at play with myself and other small boys, got a fall, by which the bone of his arm was fractured, and notwithstanding every medical aid was called for, none was availing, and amputation was recommended; but before it was executed, he died suddenly of a mortification in the wounded member.

My father, in his professional character, had a very considerable run of business, by which he supported his family handsomely, and my mother being a woman of taste and fashion they lived up to their income; consequently my father could not lay up what is called a portion for his children; but his determination was, to endeavour to give them a genteel education; and intending to bring me up to his own profession, I was early put to school, in order to acquire what was requisite, that I might at a suitable age, enter on, and go through the graduations of a classical education.

My parents, sustaining the appellation of Presbyterians had a watchful eye over my youthful morals; and although I dare not say they were at that time, acquainted with vital and experimental religion, yet every needful moral precept was inculcated; and their instruction was not lacking for the moral improvement of my mind; and having a tenacious and retentive memory, I was early instructed in the principles of the gospel according to the Presbyterian plan.

It was customary in that country and a rule among that profession, for the children and servants to attend twice a year at their kirks or meeting-houses, to have them catechised and examined by the ministers, to see what improvement they had made under the tuition and instruction of their parents and masters. And when my father sent his children and servants to undergo the examination, it was my lot to come off with approbation and praise; the minister being a tender and good man was pleased to encourage what he conceived was hopeful in me, and that before the whole congregation attending. Our neighbours would generally inform my parents of it; on which account I was much countenanced with their approbation: though then young and tender, I can now reflect back and see that, from this source, I imbibed a tolerable degree of Pharisaical pride; and possessing a tender affection for my parents, I felt my heart susceptible of receiving and desirous to pursue every moral instruction they gave me.

I cannot here refrain from making a short digression from the thread of the narrative, for since it has pleased God, I trust, to make me acquainted with vital religion and the way of salvation, through the dear Redeemer, how awful have been my sensations to discover such numbers of mankind, who having perhaps no other opportunities of instruction than I had, and possessing no more, than an orderly moral conduct, yet call themselves Christians and believers without ever being capable of giving any relation of the work of God's divine grace in their hearts, but still professing the internal evidence of having been brought home to God in the hands of a Mediator—"Having the form of Godliness, but denying the power thereof" (2 Tim 3:5); for it must be observed that those Pharisaical and self righteous persons, appear great opposers of the free, sovereign and efficacious grace of God upon the heart of a believing sinner; and the reason seems obvious, because the doctrines of divine grace, through a Redeemer, cuts out by the roots, the nerves and sinews of all their hopes, by which their enmity bursting forth, manifests itself. And on the other hand, how many thousands and tens of thousands of my poor blinded fellow creatures, are encouraged and taught to believe that there is an ability in themselves which, if exerted and improved, will bring them to a state of salvation. It is true they will (at least professionally) give credit to the grace of Christ, when the basis of the system is founded on the merit of works; neither do I think this compliment paid to Christ, is any greater than when those that blindfolded Him smote Him on the face, and said, "Prophesy unto us, who it was that smote Thee" (Luke 22:64). But to return to my own history; and contemplating the scenes that transpired in my infantile years, perhaps I then went on this principle, as far as numbers of them have done who, deceiving themselves, suppose they have found Christ—A short narrative of which I will here give.

From my parents instruction and encouragement, I imbibed a hatred against taking the name of God in vain; when I have gone in the streets of Edinburgh, which city was the place of my nativity, to play with my companion, and chanced to hear any of them take the name of

God in vain, I would put my fingers in my ears and absent myself from their company. I statedly observed the duty of prayer by myself both morning and evening; I felt an affection to hear preaching, or week day evening lectures, which induced my father to procure me a seat, that I might attend the same. I became exceedingly desirous to read the scriptures, more especially, the moving historical passages; such as Joseph in the pit and his sufferings, and Abraham offering up his son Isaac; but more particularly the life, sufferings, and death of our Lord Jesus Christ. Seeing things only with a natural eye, I viewed His sufferings only as those of a human person; and my heart being very susceptible of tender impressions, pitying and sympathizing with Him in His sufferings, it was often with difficulty that I could preserve the leaves of the book, where these mournful scenes were recorded, from the streams of tears, that flowed from my eyes.

I was also much affected, at reading the parable of the rich man and Lazarus; my belief then was, that all such voluptuous livers went to hell, and that all beggars went to heaven. The influence this belief had upon me was (as my parents did not permit me to sit at the table with them until I could behave politely before company, and the table which I occupied was in another room) that when a beggar or beggars called at the door for alms, at the season when I was at dinner, I would take up my plate with the victuals and go to the door and give it to him or them; I would not permit a servant in the house to take it from me and carry it, but would go myself and give it. The usual return the beggars made was, "The Lord bless you;" and possessing the belief that all that description of people went to heaven, I concluded God would indeed bless me and bring me there also.

There was a place on a walk, between the city of Edinburgh and the large seaport town of Leith, handsomely constructed for people to walk from the city to the town, where numbers of beggars placed themselves at certain distances from each other in order to beg from those that passed by; when I possessed a little money, that I could call my own, I would walk along that path and count how many beggars were there; then go and lay out my little stock in bread and distribute it among them according to their number, from the motive above mentioned, believed from their saying "God bless you," that the Lord would do it on their account.

About this time Mr. George Whitefield came to Edinburgh and preached morning and evening every day in the week, for several months successively, at a place called the Orphan Hospital; as several thousands attended him daily, both morning and evening, the collections, which were usually gathered at every sermon, was appropriated to the benefit of the poor orphans. I have every reason to believe the ministry of Mr. Whitefield was instrumental in converting my father to the saving knowledge of Christ; he attended his ministry every day both morning and evening, and on the Lord's Day would have his family and servants attend with him. I might here give a relation of what I called my father's conversion, with the reasons which induced me to believe it was a work of grace in the heart; but as I am not writing the history of his life, but that of my own, I shall add no more on the subject.

Chapter 2

The Author is now sent to Latin school, where were several hundreds of pupils, noblemen and gentlemen's sons, etc., among whom were a number of wild youths; his natural religion soon vanished, and he became a proficient in vain amusements.

It being a time of war with France, a military ardour took place among a number of youths in the school—he takes to boxing with some of his school mates and comes off victorious—was very seldom corrected by his Latin teachers for not getting his lessons, but pretty frequently for his mischief—when leaving the classes, his most affectionate companion entered into the naval service of his country and became a midshipman—his gold laced hat, regimentals, sword, etc., excited in our author a glow of ambition, and made him wish for such a commission.

The time at length arrived that I should go to the Latin School; at this seminary five teachers were employed in the instruction of the students entered there, and it required the term of five years to progress through the various degrees to complete their classical education. The number of pupils sometimes amounted to several hundreds, consisting of noblemen and gentlemen's sons and others, from various parts of the kingdom, and among them a number of wild youths. Here I had not fortitude sufficient to support my religion, and it was but a short time before it vanished like the morning cloud and the early dew; my natural religion soon became extinct in me, having no other basis or foundation but nature, from which it sprang.

I soon fell in with the general courses my fellow students took pleasure in, and become a very great proficient in their amusements. One thing indeed, caused a conflict between duty and inclination; my

father took some degree of pains to direct my conduct with my school
mates that I might avoid a harsh and quarrelsome conduct among them;
and having a considerable flow of natural spirit, I could hardly brook
insult; but in adhering to his directions I had to put up with repeated
insults from my school fellows: a circumstance however soon occurred,
which with some expressions accidently heard from my father's lips,
when in conversation with one of his neighbours respecting me,
produced a complete revolution in my mind and conduct afterwards.

   To explain the circumstance, it will be necessary to observe that
the nation was then at war with France, and victory attending the
British arms, through every quarter of the globe, it aroused the spirit of
the nation in a general manner; after farther conquest and the splendid
scenes of military parade that passed before our eyes, such as recruiting
parties, with martial music, camps forming in the environs, and French
prisoners marching through the streets of the city to their places of
confinement; and withal an invasion by the enemy much talked of,
infused a similar spirit of military ardour among the boys of my own age
and description. They would form little companies among themselves,
appoint their officers, and attempt to imitate discipline. My father at
that time had a clerk whose name was C__ F__; this man having a
family, and their residence at some distance, was obliged to be
frequently with them; my father dispatched me with a message for the
clerk to come to him immediately, as his presence was then necessary;
but I had scarcely proceeded one hundred yards from our own house
before I was laid hold on, by one of these little parties of recruiting
boys; and to carry on their little manoevres, they pretended I was a
deserter, and arrested me as if they intended carrying me to what they
called their guard house. I plead the message I was going upon, and
begged of them to let me pass; they laughingly said they would not, my
spirit and temper got raised, and whether I had a stick in my own hand
or wrested one from some of them I do not now recollect; but I
immediately engaged them; some of the merchants, door neighbours to
my father, stopped the people as they were passing until I cleared
myself of incumbrance. It was a scene of mirth to the spectators, and I
proceeded on my errand, delivered the message, and returned home.

The encomiums passed on me for this display of prowess reached my father's ears, and shortly afterwards, when some of his neighbours were in social conversation with him, I accidently passed the room door, and overhearing a few words of their conversation, discovered that it was about me, which prompted my curiosity to listen a little longer; when I found it was about the circumstance above related. I will not venture to relate my father's words verbatim at this distance of time, but can give the real meaning of them, which was to this effect; he knew that James possessed a spirit that needed no encouragement to prompt it on, but was better pleased to hear how he acted, than if he had ran away like a coward. I drew encouragement from these words not to put up with the insults from my school mates as I had formerly done.

The scholars of the different classes in the seminary had imbibed a portion of the martial spirit, that pervaded the nation, and it was not uncommon for them in the hours of play, or intermission, to retire to secreted places, and with apparent good humour, challenge each other to fight. They would bargain not to strike above the breath, for fear the master, should discover what they had been about; and they, in consequence, feel the rod of correction for transgressing the school discipline. It was truly remarkable to observe the good humour, they would exhibit towards each other, and the friendly manner in which they would return at the appointed hour to attend their instructions.

The circumstances attending my conduct in never joining in their exercises, appeared to me cowardly; and I had no doubt but my school fellows considered me as destitute of courage; but the encouragement I took from my father's expression disposed me not to appear so in future; and an opportunity soon occurred which brought my resolution to the test. One of my school mates, when a number of us were playing together, told me before all, that if I would fight him he would tie one of his hands behind his back: I accepted his challenge, and our action did not continue more than half a minute, before he gave over the contest; I then challenged him, allowing him both his hands at liberty; but the second combat was as short as the first. Growing somewhat elated, I then proposed tying one of my hands and fighting him with the other; whether this last proposal was accepted or not, I cannot positively determine.

This circumstance in some measure, impressed my school mates with the idea that I was not a coward; and from my success I grew fond of, and took pleasure in the practice of boxing, until I became a great proficient in the unbecoming art, which was too prevalent among the major part of those attending our school. However I got a shock, in consequence of one of my rencounters, which in a measure blunted the edge of my desires, and cured my propensity of engaging in that practice again, at least for a time. The occurrence was as follows: a few gentlemen's sons with myself who were recreating ourselves in the evening, at a retired place from the city, concluded we could not part without trying our manhood or boyhood with each other: I proposed to engage three of them at once, of equal size with myself, provided they would stretch a rope between us: they laughing, told me I could not undertake two such ones, pointing them out. I agreed to their proposal, and the preliminaries were adjusted, but in the commencement one of my antagonists got his thumb put out of place which of course ended the combat.

One of our company then present was a son of Lord Huntingdon, and some of our comrades insisted I was not able to try him alone; he was older, larger grown, and stronger built than myself, but I accepted the proposal and the combat immediately began; after a severe conflict between us, I came off victor, and he was taken sick in a short time afterwards. Physicians attended him, he being incapable of attending the classes. On being informed of his situation, a transport of fear seized me, lest I should be the effect of what passed between us: my fears ran so far as to make me apprehend, that if he died his father being one of the Lords, that tried criminals for capital crimes, I might be brought to die for him.

I can hardly remember ever receiving any correction from my Latin teacher for neglect in not having my lesson, or for being a dunce, but often was subjected to severe corrections for my wildness and wickedness. Every master had his school room on the second floor distinct from each other, and each room was large and capacious: when the scholars would be getting their lessons, before silence was commanded, and to come forward and rehearse them at the master's chair, it was usual for the teacher to walk backwards and forwards the

length of the school room, for the benefit of exercise and a nearer
scrutiny to the attention of the pupils; in order to make sport for the
rest, as soon as he would turn from me, I would get up, under pretence
to ask the English of a Latin word, and as the teacher wore a large wig
curled and powdered, I would hold up my book close to the hinder part
of his wig, that he might not see what I was about, when at the same
instant I was beating the powder out of the curls of his wig with my
fingers: sometimes I would pretend to be footing of him with my foot
projected before me; he would soon perceive from the actions and
smiling of the scholars, that something [I] was doing that was not right,
and wheeling about on his heel, would detect me in the very action, the
certain consequence of which was, that I was subjected to what I then
called a severe chastisement, but which I have long since been
convinced I justly merited by my conduct. However, I began to imbibe
a prejudice against learning; and if complaints to my parents, without
their inquiring into the cause, would have taken me from school, such
complaints would not have been wanting on my part. But my parents
were proof against suffering their children to bring home any complaint
against their teacher, knowing him to be a gentleman of humanity,
probity, and good conduct, and that his actions were in conformity
therewith: If therefore, I merited chastisement, as it was my wildness
and folly that subjected me to it, I had to lay my account to bear it, and
although conceived heart prejudices against my teacher at the time I
suffered these chastisements, yet as my reason grew a little stronger it
wore away, and when I left school none loved him more affectionately
than I did.

Some of my most affectionate companions at school were sons of
those celebrated—Mr. Erskine's, faithful and pious ministers of
Scotland. Some persuasions may talk of federal holiness, that holy
parents will beget holy children, that if the root be holy the branches
are holy also: but although these young men could have boasted of as
pious parents as any in the kingdom, yet there appeared in them as little
federal holiness as in the wildest students at the seminary.

When we left the classes my most affectionate companion, Mr.
Erskine's son, chose to prefer a life in the naval service of his country;
the first station conferred upon youths of family and character on board

of a ship of war, is that of a midshipman; and when I beheld my friend with his gold laced hat, a sword by his side, and clothed in his regimentals, being naturally myself of a martial turn, I felt a glow of ambition, wishing that I could obtain an equal commission. It was the pride of life and dress that had influence with me, more than any service I could render to my country at my years.

Chapter 3

Mr. Ireland's father sends him a coasting voyage to London to try how the sea would agree with his constitution—nothing material happens on this voyage, except a moderate storm, and the loss of their cable and anchor—his uncle George then lived in London—he had a comfortable passage home—takes a second voyage in the winter season—a hot press for seamen in London on their arrival there—the mate, not having a protection, he acts in his place on shore—a violent storm takes place, on their homeward bound voyage, which continued thirty-two hours; and although he expected immediate death, yet no sense of the unpreparedness of his soul for eternity did he feel during this time—one consequence of said storm was, their ship became leaky, and in entering a harbour she ran upon rocks which rendered her much more so; in consequence of which, they narrowly escaped going to the bottom.

My father discovering my inclination, although not agreeable to his wishes, was pleased to send me a coasting voyage to London upon trial, to discover how the sea would agree with my constitution. The commander of the ship was my father's relation, by whom I was treated perhaps with a greater degree of tenderness than if it had been otherwise: I lived as my captain did, for he generally would supply himself and the cabin passengers with every comfortable necessary, that could be obtained from the towns along the shore.

Nothing material occurred on our passage excepting what the sailors called a moderate storm; we came to an anchor in the evening about seven or eight leagues from the mouth of the Thames, and it blew very rough all night with a tolerable high sea before us; in the morning the man of war that was convoy to our fleet, hove out a signal for the fleet to heave their anchors and follow him; we made the attempt, with all the force of the male passengers on board as well as the sailors, to get our anchors up but could not; and to obey the signal we were obliged to slip our cables, and leave them and the anchors behind; however we soon got to our destined port.

I had some near connections in London; my uncle George, whom my grandfather disinherited resided in that city; his two eldest sons had embraced a military life, and the elder of the two was then in the King's life guards; what commission he bore I could not ascertain; but by his uniform it appeared to be an office of consequence. The pleasure I had in visiting my connections, with the general curiosities about London, together with a comfortable passage home again, made it a very pleasant voyage to me.

Shortly after our arrival at home, my parents applied to our relation, the captain, to know what they were indebted for my trial voyage. He answered them nothing, provided they would let me go a winter voyage to London with him; by which it would be better known whether the sea would agree with me or not; to which they consented. I set off with him the second voyage, and although we had rough and winter weather, nothing worthy of notice occurred on our passage, and we arrived in safety at our desired port. At that period the press for seamen was very hot in London, and few persons that could be caught on shore without a protection, escaped being pressed and sent on board men of war. The second in command, in our ship, was the captain's relation as well as myself, and we two were bedfellows, but he had not protection; the ship having taken in part of her cargo, moved off to the middle of the stream; but as part of our cargo remained to be taken in, and the mate not having a protection dared not appear on shore, in consequence of the press, the captain entrusted me with the execution of the duty of the mate, in receiving the goods, passing receipts therefore, and having them put into the warehouse. A certain emolument was attached to the execution of these duties, which of right belonged to the mate; and as I discharged his services on shore he agreed to divide the profit with me; from the warehouse the goods were conveyed in lighters to the ship in the stream.

Receiving intelligence that the fleet homeward bound must be at Sheer-ness at a given period, as the man of war, which was to guard it from French privateers, would be ready to sail at such a time, our ship did not complete her lading: the last part of the cargo we put on board was a quantity of sugar, probably about sixty Hogsheads, when we dropped down the river Thames to meet our convoy at the appointed time and place.

Nothing worthy of notice transpired among the fleet during almost three fourths of our voyage homeward; but when we came opposite to a place called Tinmouth Castle or Tinmouth Bay we were, in the evening, arrested by a violent hurricane off the shore; had the hurricane been in shore the whole fleet, to appearance, must inevitably have been dashed to pieces. The storm increasing, all hands were engaged in furling the sails, as no vessel dared to show a bit of canvass but at the expense of being torn to pieces. I was struck with wonder, not only at the length of time it took to hand our fore-sail that was up in the braces, but more so that every individual, was not swept off the yards arm into the sea, as it would often come over their heads as if they were enveloped in it, and the next flap would whirl them all in the great deep; but under a kind and providential hand we were all preserved. Our ship being now under blunt poles (as the seamen phrase it) we lashed the helm hard a lee, then proceeded to get the hatch-ways all put down with tarpolans over them, and the bars and bolts fixed to keep them down, in order to prevent the water from getting into the hold, as the sea was continually breaking in upon us.

There were none above deck but the captain, carpenter and myself; the rest being all confined below, and the ship left to the mercy of the waves—a dismal night indeed we had of it; and the farther the ship was drove from the shore, the more awful, and tremendous the waves seemed to roll. When day light returned the skies were clear, no clouds intercepting the rays of the sun, but still the hurricane continued in its utmost force, and the waves, according to the sea phrase, rolled mountains high. The seas that broke in upon us, tore away our quarter rails, and certain bales of goods that had been fastened to them, that were not subject to damage by water, we now saw floating in the sea.

The awful rolling of the ship, which as has been observed, was not fully loaded, started the sugar Hogsheads, that being the upper part of the lading, to one side, which gave the ship a considerable keel in the water; and the vessel beginning to be a little leaky when she would right, between the waves, the carpenter with myself, would add a few strokes to the pump, when to the best of my recollection, I had to lash myself to the shrouds with the lower end of the main top sail halliards, to prevent my falling overboard.

I must acknowledge, that during this hurricane which continued about thirty-two hours, although I conceived every roll the ship gave she would turn keel up and plunge us down to the bottom of the ocean, yet I never had possessed during the whole storm, the least sense of the unpreparedness of my soul for eternity; and no thought of heaven or hell, God or Devil, as far as I can recollect, ever entered into my mind. Our fleet were all scattered with not more than two ships then in view; the elements appeared as if they were in a flame, through the violence of the wind carrying some particles of the surge in to the air, and the reflection of the sun, shining through the bespangled atmosphere, made it appear like flame to our view. All the thoughts I then had, respecting my situation which only passed through mind without leaving any solemn impression was, that provided, I was once more placed on shore, I would suffer my two ears to be cut off if I ever ventured again on the ocean—So hardened, and wretched a situation was I then in. However, towards the end of the storm, the wind considerably abated and veered round from the course it was. Being now more in our favour, we unlashed the helm from hard a weather, and got it up to hard a lee; and with the help of our gib or the fore-stay sail, we wore the ship round, and got her lee side against the course from which the waves come; which in a little time hove back that part of the cargo which had started, almost to its old birth again, which nearly righted the ship until daylight came, to enable us to act with more safety to ourselves, in completing the same.

The man of war who conveyed us, was so racked in the storm, as I was informed, that he was obliged to reduce his metal from nine to six pounders: and perceiving the fleet all dispersed, he pressed all the sail he could carry, pursued his voyage, and left us to shift for ourselves.

We never heard of the loss of any of the fleet save one that was cast away; and ours not being yet in a safe situation from French privateers, all hands exerted themselves to spread all the canvass we dared to carry, and continued our exertions day and night until we arrived in sight of our intended port and desired haven; when we pressed with all the sail we could carry in order to get early that evening into the harbour; the mouth of which we were just entering when daylight left us, and looking up towards my native city of Edinburgh, the high street of which is conspicuous, the city being built on a hill, and beholding the windows with lighted candles in them, where, if I did not see the residence of my own parents, I was certain I saw others contiguous to it; my heart was elated with the idea, that in about two hours I would be at my father's house; at which period our ship ran aground—We fired a signal gun for a pilot which came immediately off to us, and informed us the tide would rise about two feet higher when throwing our top sails aback, the vessel floated immediately, and we informed the pilots we would stand a little off to sea, and if the tide rose to the height they mentioned, they should hoist two lamps upon the light house as a signal to us, and we would tack about and stand in for the harbour. When the lamps were hoisted we were too far off to recover our distance before the ebb would commence; and our ship being very leaky, our captain concluded to stand for another harbour on the opposite side of that prong or arm of the sea, called Brunt Island, because it drew a greater depth of water.

There was what was called a pier, projecting a tolerable distance out into the sea, at the end of which the light house was fixed to direct vessels into the harbour; it was in a triangular form, and attending the light house, at the time of the stream tides which happened there at the full and change of the moon, being considered hazardous. While we were at London it had been removed into the middle angle, which we were ignorant of, and pressing with a full sail for the harbour, being guided by the lamp at the light house, we got into danger before we were aware; and before the ship could be wore around, she struck upon the rocks several times, which sprung some awful leaks in our vessel. Had she been drove off any distance from the harbour, whoever would have perished or escaped, the ship must have gone to the bottom; for as we entered the harbour she was filling fast with water, and the tide then ebbing, we ran her aground and got assistance from the town to double man the pumps, in order to empty her of water, which in process of time was accomplished; and the carpenters with lights, applied themselves to stopping the leaks which was done as well as time and circumstances would admit of. In about two weeks we could venture across to our native harbour. The damage the ship sustained, rendered it necessary to have her bottom new sheathed from the keel up to the bends all over. This was the end of my second voyage: but not after impression was made of the awful danger I had escaped.

Chapter 4

The author's design is rather to contract, than go into minute details; he cannot pass by some imminent dangers through which he was brought, in order to set forth the wonderful goodness of God, etc., such as falling twice through the ice, and narrowly escaping drowning, - touches on the many perils attending his three voyages to Greenland a whale catching, and the many wonders in those northern seas—relates one more instance of imminent danger, attending one of those voyages.

It is not my design, to swell the relation of this narrative with every circumstance of danger that I have escaped: my intention is to contract rather than go into the minutia of detail; but I cannot help recording some imminent dangers through which I have been brought, in order to set forth the wonderful goodness of God; whose watchful providence was superintending my safety, when I had not His fear before my eyes, but seemed bent on doing mischief and wickedness. My purpose, however, is to be very brief on any farther circumstances that attended me in Europe, except in the two or three instances following.

On the north side of the City of Edinburgh there is a lengthy body of water called the North Locke; winters are sometimes severe in that climate, and when the ice was capable of bearing any number of people those among all ranks, who were fond of a practice called skating, would repair from the city to the Locke for their amusement: perhaps there was boundaries sufficient for twelve or fifteen hundred to exercise themselves in. The first adventurers were generally thoughtless lads who seeing no danger, feared none; which at times terminated in the drowning of these unwary youths.

I was generally myself one of these forward adventurers, and once sustained a heavy shock at seeing one of my comrades who fell in, drawn up dead with a small grappling iron, which had caught in his nostrils. The screams of the mother and the amiableness of the youth produced a considerable degree of sorrow among the hundreds who were attending on shore and beheld the unhappy spectacle. The impression was but momentary on my mind, although ere long I was subjected to a visitation by a like casualty which, had it not been for the providence of God that preserved me, must have terminated in a like catastrophe with myself. A number were sliding from the edge of the Locke towards the middle, when the ice not being sufficiently strong to bear us up, myself and a few others, that were standing with me, all went down together; the shore was crowded with spectators, and the general cry was for ropes to be conveyed to us that we might, by tying them about us, be drawn out of the water, as we supported ourselves upon the edge of the ice with our hands, but could not extricate ourselves from our perilous situation. In process of time the ropes were brought and by the assistance of the numbers, who beheld the spectacle, the ends of them were conveyed to us which we were drawn out of our danger and delivered from any future apprehensions.

Another circumstance of danger attended me on the same waters; when going across about the centre of the Locke, which was pretty wide, in order to put on my skates, at which practice I was very expert, having a thinner piece of ice to go over than was expected, I all on a sudden fell in, my feet went foremost and my body followed nearly in a floating position; when my head got under the water and under the ice, I had the presence of mind to throw my arms backwards and caught the edge of the ice, through which I went down, almost by the first joints of my fingers, by which my body was drawn back to the hole, and so escaped the danger. Had I missed that hold, to every appearance, I must have finally drowned, as no one was near to aid or relieve me.

But the greatest of all dangers I ever was exposed to happened in the north seas, on an outward bound passage to Greenland. Meaning to omit a variety of matter that perhaps might entertain if related, I shall confine myself to this one circumstance in Europe. Whether my father intended my voyage to Greenland for the purpose of producing an aversion in me again going to sea, I cannot, at present, absolutely determine; but it so happened, that I went three voyages which I shall contract into the recital of the one instance before me. If his intention was to frighten me from the sea, he certainly took a wrong method, as the sequel will show.

There were four ships that went a whale catching in company together from Leith; all which were considered as subject to the command of a Commodore. I had but one near relation who had any command in these ships, and [as] he did not sail in the ship I did, of course could be of no service to me. But I had a near connection who was part owner of that fleet or squadron, and superintended every thing relative to the ships, both as to victualing and paying the men their wages. What communication passed between my father and him I did not hear, but am fully persuaded it was of the tender kind towards me, as the voyage was considered, both severe and dangerous; he also introduced, a degree of acquaintance and friendship with the Commodore, whose name was Yan Yonson, a Hollander, a gentle and humane man; he visited at my father's, which reconciled my parents the better to this voyage, as I was to sail with him; and indeed I was treated by him with all the humanity of a father, and he entrusted me with the care of all his stores, with which he was bountifully supplied, and enjoyed the use of every thing designed for him.

My airy, antic and volatile spirit soon gained me the affection of the officers, and I also became the favourite of the sailors. Was it requisite, I might here give an account of the many wonders of God I saw in the great deep whilst in those northern regions—of the many cajolate whales we saw in the north seas; of the gradual diminution of the night as we drew nearer the coasts of Spitsbergen, until we arrived at perfect day and constant sunshine, excepting the interposition of clouds, snow, or rainy weather; of the huge fish called Fin-fish, and as we were advancing farther among the ice of the many seals we saw and caught, of the large white Bear, walking on the ice and swimming from one piece to another; and when we pressed them with a view to catch them, would jump from the ice, dive under the water and come up along side of our boat for the purpose of attacking us. There we saw the Sea Horse; the taking of whom is attended with so much difficulty and

danger; they are amphibious creatures, with immense long white teeth.
We also saw the beautiful unicorn fish, spotted over like calico, with a
large white straight horn projecting from its forehead outwards; some of
which are computed from six to eight and nine feet in length—These
with various other views, of sixty or seventy ships, when the wind was at
southeast blowing us to the northwest, all frozen up near each other for
the space of several weeks; and while in that situation, we discovered a
number of men walking on the ice to the amount of six or eight in
company, whose strong new ship had been crushed to pieces by two
large flounces of ice, coming up against each other and catching her
between them: and when they got to our ship we hoisted a flag at the
foretop mast head as a signal that they had got on board—This
encouraged the rest to take their tracks, and follow their forlorn ship
mates, from one piece of ice to another, until they all arrived in safety,
without injury to any one individual.

These circumstances, some of which excited pleasure and others
admiration, together with some danger which I, with others, was
exposed to, in catching whales, I now finally pass by, and return to that
instance of imminent danger hinted at above. We were pretty far
advanced in the north seas, on our voyage outward bound, and had been
visited with a storm, whether a violent or moderate one, I will not
determine; but as a storm in those seas produces a very lofty swell in the
waves subsequent to its termination, we were becalmed almost in an
instant; and although the wind was favourable, yet there was not a
sufficient breeze to undulate the water so as to work the ship, we had
not then got up our top-gallant-yards, but concluded to improve the
calm, in order to have them fixed up, with a view, as there was an
appearance of moderate weather, to spread all the canvass we could, in
order to expedite our voyage.

Men unacquainted with the sea cannot form an adequate judgment
what a sweep through the air a person at the top-gallant-mast-head must
experience in a ship of four hundred tons burden, becalmed and rolling
from side to side by a heavy sea. When our ship was in this situation the
boatswain addressed himself to several young men in language similar to
this; "Which of you, my active young lads, will venture up to the top-
gallant-mast-head, taking with you the top-gallant block, in order to

reeve the rope belonging to the block through the sheave, and fasten the end of it to the ring at the main-top-mast-head? Then we will get the top-gallant halliards reeved, hoist the top-gallant-yard and have it slung to the mast."

I immediately sprung forward, and offered my service to perform it; up I went with apparent alacrity; the higher I got, I found it necessary to be the more cautious, in consequence of the rolling of the ship. When I had ascended to the main-top-mast-head and looked above me to the top-gallant-mast, I found there were very few ratlings fixed to the main-top-gallant-mast-shrouds (which ratlings serve as a ladder for sailors to mount aloft by) so that I had to perform the other distance, by what the sailors call shinning it up. When I got to my destined spot and untied the rope to run it through the sheave, the block dropped out of my hand, and miraculously indeed was I preserved from falling—Once I think for a few moments, my legs got untwisted from the shrouds, and my whole weight was suspended by one hand; I, however, executed the task I had voluntarily undertaken to do, and descended down to the quarter-deck. When I was aloft, I dared not look down to the ship for fear the gazing company should shew a sudden surprise; neither dared they call aloft to me for fear of my doing the same.

When I got safe on deck and began to view the danger I had been in, I was seized with an immediate panic, and shook all over as if I had been in an ague. Of all the dangers I ever was exposed to, I humbly conceive this was the greatest; and my escape and deliverance from it the most singular. Natural fears at times would attend me when I reflected on it; but no sense of gratitude to my great Preserver. How suitably was that passage adapted to my sensations in Rom. 8:7, "The carnal mind is enmity against God, it is not subject to the law of God neither indeed can be." As also Psalm 58:3, "The wicked are estranged from the womb, they go astray as soon as they are born, speaking lies."

From thence we proceeded on our voyage home, and shortly after I embarked for America. The circumstances which lead to my embarkation for this country, and final separation from my parents, friends, and native land, are of themselves, of a nature, at this time probably of not sufficient magnitude to detail; suffice it say, they arose from an act of juvenile indiscretion, and the rigor of the penal laws of the government under which I was born and raised. I however, hailed my removal[12] as the most auspicious and fortunate epoch of my life. It pleased my Great Deliverer to bring good out of evil, and I was destined to exchange a land of tyranny and sanguinary oppression, for a country of liberty, reason, and humanity.

True it is, that on my first arrival in Virginia, and for a few years after, this now happy country too, groaned under the tyranny of a rigorous religious intolerance: but it soon pleased the great Giver of all good, through the instrumentality of the revolution, to burst asunder the bands of tyranny, and I was permitted, with all others to enjoy that entire freedom of conscience, in the exercise of my ministry, in the gospel of a blessed Redeemer, so congenial and balmy to the human mind—From this rigorous intolerance arose many of my severe trials and cruel persecutions in the early part of my gospel labours, which will be detailed in their proper place.

---

[12] Note by the editor of the 1819 edition: "A more conclusive evidence, we presume, the author of this work could not have given, of his being under the influence of divine grace, and of being a true servant of God, than is exhibited in the above brief sketch of the circumstance that brought him to this country—Like the ancient people of God, he does not design to keep out of sight his sin, but with them, in the biography of their lives, he exposes to public view his imperfections and blemishes as well as the fair side of his character; and like the excellent John Newton, he is desirous of 'showing the world how far the free and sovereign grace of God has been extended in the salvation of a sinner' —although we are warranted in saying that the cause itself which procured his banishment from his native country was of so trivial a nature as would not have produced the most gentle reproof from one in a thousand of the citizens of America."

Chapter 5

In this chapter the author relates a remarkable and alarming dream he had, which produced strange reflections and a partial reformation in him, for a short time—In consequence of an application, he removes near forty miles, and sets in to teaching school there—The people with few exceptions, are very wicked—He falls in with a religious friend, the initials of whose name was N. F. who was, in time, made the instrument of religious impressions on his mind; and before whom, from his first acquaintance, he could not carry on his wickedness with freedom. A striking instance of this is given—He hears of and goes to see a countryman of his, etc.

Soon after I came to America, I had a singular dream which produced some momentary effects upon me at that time, which were as follows, viz. I dreamt that I was walking in the high street of the city of my nativity, and the Devil appeared to me, and in an instant, laid hold of my person and, as I thought, carried me down bodily to hell. It appeared to me that the entrance therein was by two large leafed gates; and as he opened the gates in order to thrust me in, I felt as if an awful steam of heat issued therefrom; before he could execute his purpose however, I was bound fast under the arm pits by a long silver cord, the end of which reached to heaven, and I was in an instant delivered, and sat down upon the spot, where the grand enemy seized me. The dream was repeated a number of times in my sleep, without any alteration of circumstance attending the first; and as often as I was carried down by Satan, so often was I relieved and delivered by that silver cord from heaven. How many times the dream was repeated I cannot recollect at present; but when I awoke and reflected upon it, it produced some strange sensations in me.

I dare not say it left any impressions of my guilty state, but it produced in me a partial reformation, for about a week.

After I had recovered from my last stroke of affliction, a stranger lodged all night at my place of residence, who lived about thirty-six or forty miles from there; who, among other subjects of conversation, informed the family that he was in search of a schoolmaster, who would meet with ample encouragement in the parts where he lived, provided he was capable to teach, and could come well recommended. Not being there that night myself, they recommended me to him, and upon their recommendation he offered encouragement for me to go to his house; and, as they told me, spoke so highly of himself that they conceived him to be a leading character in those parts. However, when I went up I found it quite the reverse, but at the same time, was informed that the settlement stood much in need of a teacher among them. I applied to one of the most reputable characters in the neighborhood, who soon collected a few of his nearest neighbors, that wished to encourage a school; and after proving me a little, and requesting me to write a line or two before them, they appeared well pleased, and every thing was fixed to the satisfaction of both parties, and the school was to commence on a certain day; at which time I attended, and commenced immediately; and so on obtained an acquaintance with the temper disposition and practice of the settlement which produced a very considerable shock in my mind, by comparing the contrast between the people amongst whom I had lived and those amongst whom, I was now to live.

Although I had very little of the fear of God before my eyes if any, yet from the benefit of an early education and parental instruction, together with the practice of those amongst whom I had lived, I felt some degree of reverence of the Lord's Day. In my new settlement there was not the least appearance of respect for the Sabbath excepting amongst a few Quakers, who on the first day of the week, would meet a certain house and pursue their modes according to their way of thinking. It was the only day of general sport, merriment and dissipation in the vicinity where I resided; and no scenes of vanity or wickedness, would they hesitate to pursue, or practice. When I beheld their practice, the first influence it had upon me was, that it disposed me to take my Bible and retire into the woods by myself, where I spent a good part of the day in reading; and to the best of my recollection, I wept and prayed also; why I wept or prayed I cannot remember, but rather impute it, however, to spontaneous acts in me, (as I can assign no rational or moral cause for my exercise) arising from a sudden shock, their practice gave me, for it left no impression of sin and guilt upon my conscience.

Those partial Lord's Day impressions soon "vanished like the morning cloud and the early dew." Not many weeks passed before I could heartily join with them in all their wicked amusements without remorse; and being of an aspiring disposition, it did not suit my taste to be a common accomplice with them in their vices, but also an active head or leader in every practice of wickedness, so that it might be said of me as in Isaiah 5:18, "I drew iniquity with the cords of vanity and sin as with a cart rope." During the year that I resided in those parts, I cannot recollect that ever I experienced any remorse of conscience excepting in one instance; so wretched, seared and hardened had I got to be. One instance of vice I would relate, as something singular attended it were it not that I can conceive my dissolution fast approaching, which obliges me to hasten on to matters of greater importance. A few circumstances I shall mention during my residence there relative to a person, the initials of whose name was N. F.[13] as I shall be obliged to bring him in, the sequel, being instrumental in the hands of God, towards the first impressions that were made upon my soul. There were two characters that I possessed a veneration for at all times, the first, where I conceived a man, acting in the sacred function, to be a good man. The other a professor of religion, when I entertained a belief he possessed what he professed. It is a fixed principle with me, where a man professes religion, and carries the fear of God daily before his eyes, it will display a native grandeur, dignity and majesty, so far as to command a degree of respect in the breasts of wicked men, by which they are in some measure awed from going on so boldly in their wickedness in their presence, as they would have done, had they been absent. This was the

---

[13] According to Garnett Ryland, N. F. is Nicholas Fane. See Garnett Ryland, "James Ireland: An Address by Garnett Ryland Delivered at the Unveiling of the Monument to James Ireland, May 20, 1931." Richmond: The Virginia Baptist Historical Society\University of Richmond, 1931, p. 5.

case with respect to myself, alluding to the person mentioned above. I was persuaded he was a good man, and feared God; which had such an influence upon me that I could not go on with my wickedness in his presence, as well as if he had been absent.

Being invited to a certain gentleman's house to what is called a husking, and being divided in different parties, he made choice to be close by me, and the general subject that he was upon, was briefly about religion; as he told me afterwards, I was a youth that might be led, but could not be drove, and possessing some strange and unusual impressions towards me, which at that time he said he could not account for, led him [to] come from the city and place of my nativity, with to make that subject a topic between us. Every ingratiating method that he could take, he pursued in order to acquire my confidence. It happened when we were conversing together, that a man who conceived himself pretty active in dissipation and burlesque, was running blackguard upon the rest of the company; I was all on nettle to be at him, but this good man's presence had such an awe upon me, that I could not encounter the other, whilst standing along side of him; for a few minutes I avoided his company, and retired, in order to engage the other, and caused some of my companions to form a line between that good man and me, in order to prevent him from seeing what I was about. I then got upon my knees to prevent being seen, encountered this wicked champion, and run him aground in a few minutes. I only mention this in order to show what commanding influence the presence of a gracious man will have over a wicked person's conduct at such a period.

After having executed my purpose I returned to his company immediately, he very well knew my voice, and heard what I was about, yet never made the least mention of it to me. He appeared to have a most ingratiating and insinuating manner of address, which acquired an insensible influence over me that evening. The next opportunity I had of seeing him, was on a Lord's Day, in going to make inquiry after a person who I had been informed had lately a view that I might obtain, perhaps, some information relative to my parents. I met with N. F. in my way thither, he appeared affectionately pleased to see me, addressed me in the kindest terms, and lovingly took me by the hand, inquired after my welfare; to which I replied in a friendly manner, with inquiry after himself and other connections; putting my hand in my pocket I complimented him with some very good peaches; not being disposed for religious converse at that time, and being eager to pursue my inquiry, turned about to my companion and challenged him to run our horses a quarter in his presence, which my companion assented to. I politely bid my friend farewell, and started in the race immediately. What plain indications were my actions, of the wickedness and wretchedness of my heart. I found the person I was in search of, and also found he belonged to a family with whom my father's family maintained a friendly intercourse. He was ten years in advance above my age, yet I was extremely glad to see him, from repeated information I received from him, and as he acquired both respect and esteem in that neighborhood. I shall leave him at present, until I bring him in again under particular circumstances.

Chapter 6

The author visited those parts frequently where his acquaintance lived, it was a settlement much abandoned to pleasures, pastimes and profanity—He is esteemed a complete dancer among them—They want a schoolmaster in that settlement, apply to, and get him to come down and teach for them—Remorse of conscience becomes a stranger to him, and he thinks he would not exchange his present pleasures in sin for the happiness of the saints above—Notwithstanding his vanity and wickedness, he kept good orders in his school—He was tempted to disbelieve the being of God—was much employed in making songs and satirical compositions—his friend N. F. prevails on him to make a poem on charity, or brotherly love.

Visiting these parts repeatedly, I became tolerably well acquainted with the settlement in general; and these parts were much more to my taste than the settlement in which I at that time resided. A considerable number of the people of both sexes were nearly of my age; their recreations, pleasures and pastimes, were very congenial to my wishes. Balls, dancing and chanting to the sound of the violin, was the most prevailing practice in that settlement. That being my darling idol, and being esteemed by all who ever saw me perform upon the floor, a most complete dancer; which accomplishment so called, together with my other moods of address, soon acquired me the confidence and esteem of those called, now a days, young ladies. The young men through the settlement in general, appeared to be destitute of every virtuous or moral qualification, and heads of tolerably numerous families were equally as wild and dissipated as the youth. When in companies together nothing was heard, comparatively speaking, but obscene language, cursing and swearing, drinking and frolicking, horse racing and other vices, with the exception of a few characters or families in that settlement.

Being in want of a schoolmaster, it was their general desire to have me the following year down amongst them; with the promise of generous encouragement, I soon consented. My conscience, by this time, appeared to be seared as with a hot iron; remorse was an utter stranger to my breast when I came down to live amongst them; I possessed certain qualifications by which I could accommodate myself to every company; with the religious I could moralize a little; with the well bred I could be polite; with the merry I could be antique; and with the obscene I could be profane. I may venture to say, with great propriety, that I was engaged "to treasure up unto myself wrath, against the day of wrath and revelation of the righteous judgment of God to come." The god of this world had so blinded my present understanding, that comparing my present pleasure in sin together with my confused ideas of the happiness of heaven, I often thought I would not have changed my present pleasures in sin, for the happiness of the saints above, if God would have given me to enjoy it. I truly can say, I was not only willing to be wicked, but studied to be so. Profane and jest books I procured to improve me in vice; and never could I hear a pertinent answer (as I thought) that would nonplus an opponent in folly without studying a variety of answers, in order to take them off on all occasions. I cannot help remarking what an opposite course I pursued with regard to those that were under my tuition and instruction—I would reprove sin in every one that I knew acted improperly from school; I set an orderly example before my scholars, and prided myself in a conformity to orderly and regular rule, by which I acquired a general esteem as a teacher.

I think for about six months before my religious impressions, the adversary of souls pestered my mind daily about the being and eternity of God, endeavouring to destroy the idea of an eternal Being, by bringing it to the bar of depraved reason. Could he have completed his purposes with me, I believe his design was to make me an Atheist. I was much taken up in those times with making songs and satirical poems, which had a pleasing influence on the generality of the settlement, which highly gratified me. The aforementioned good man N. F. had

seen a variety of my compositions, and was determined to address me on
the subject the first opportunity. The period was soon brought about,
when we accidentally met at two cross roads; I was going to my school
and he about his secular affairs. After an affectionate introduction on his
part, he introduced the subject in the manner following. I think, said
he, calling me his dear friend, I have seen some of your poetical
compositions. I asked him how he liked them; he replied they were well
enough for the occasions they were applied to; but told me he would
speak his mind freely, if I would not get offended at his freedom. I
replied nothing that he would say would give me offence. He then
calmly told me that all gifts came from God; and that gifts were not
grace; that I possessed gifts, but that I did not possess the grace of God;
and it was but reasonable that where God bestowed a gift, it should be
improved for Him and not in the service of the Devil.

What he said I took all in good part. He then modestly proposed, if
I would compose a poem for him, he would give a subject; to which I
consented; the subject he gave me was charity. Being well acquainted
with the common acceptation of the word charity, that it consisted in a
person's being of a free, liberal and humane disposition, with a heart and
hand open to relieve the distresses of the needy, as well as to
commiserate their wants; and believing him to be a truly good man, I
conceived that the charity he alluded to was different from my common
idea of it; but such was the pride of my heart that I would not ask him
his definition of it, lest he should discover my ignorance, and be led to
entertain a meaner opinion of my parts, than I wished him to have.
Before we parted he explained the word accidentally by saying, "My
friend the next time I see you I will expect to see your piece on charity
or brotherly love." Upon which we immediately parted.

I was then led on to a few reflections.—Having been not long
before that period, at a yearly meeting of a people, to which my
religious friend belonged, I recollected them calling each other brother,
which appellation I knew did not belong to them by blood, otherwise
than being the children of the universal family of Adam; my reflections
immediately led me to conceive they possessed a religion which united
them together in affection, and called each other brother in
consequence thereof.

Were I disposed to correct the following piece, I could make it appear more consistent with the form of sound words; but being then in my natural and wicked state, I choose, therefore, to give it in the ideas I then possessed; and as there will be a variety of compositions interspersed in my narrative, they will appear more consistent with soundness, as I became some further enlightened—The piece composed is as follows:

1

Of all the passions that's in man,
That his desires do most inflame,
Is that of love which doth control
All raptures that spring from the soul:
It conquers pride and doth assuage
The dreadful spleen of fiery rage.

2

Yet when I view infinite love
Of the eternal God above,
To us poor sinful worms on earth,
Who being in a state of death,
And by the law condemn'd to hell,
As we against Him rebel—

3

Did send His precious Son below,
To save us from eternal woe;
And in our nature suffer'd death,
And vengeance of His Father's wrath,
What the law could inflict on Him,
To make a recompense for sin.

4

Who, direct to His Father's will,
Did all the law precepts fulfill;
Instead of works, unto our race

Presents a covenant of grace;
That we by Him in this abode,
May be reconcil'd to God.

5

O! how ought this our passions move
With flowing streams of raptur'd love;
When the great God pronounces forth,
Eternal peace to us on earth;
If we by faith believe the word
Of Jesus Christ His Son, our Lord.

6

Again how ought our bowels move
In streams of sympathetic love,
To Christ the Son of God on high,
Who to redeem our souls did die;
Our faculties should be all fire
Flowing to Him with love's desire.

7

Secondly, from our love to God,
Let us return to earth's abode,
Where, if we see and doth perceive
Any that in our Lord believe,
It ought to make our bowels move
On them with a brotherly love.

8

For when our Lord He did ascend
To His Father, left this command
Unto His disciples, that they
His dictating rule might obey;
Saying "This precept I discover,
As I love you, love one another."

9

From this command we may imply
The Christian's love is not to die;
To love a servant of the Lord,
Who doth embrace His truth and word,
And let no forms us disagree
But live in love and harmony.

10

For if our church forms don't agree,
It should not blast our unity,
Whilst doctrines and our faith are one
Believing in Jesus Christ alone;
And for His sake we with each other
Should live in brotherly love together.

11

Now to the eternal God above,
Be everlasting flames of love;
And to His glorious Son on high
That sav'd us from such misery;
May all the earth these names adore
Now henceforth and forevermore.

Chapter 7

He carries the composition to his friend; joins with him in singing it: His friend approves well of it, and solicits him to make him another piece, and to choose his own subject, which is the natural man's dependence for heaven.

The poem being finished, I went to pay my friend a visit, and carried it with me. He was raising a barn that day, which obliged him to collect a number of people; when I arrived he made inquiry if I had complied with his request, on which I presented my verse immediately to him. After reading them over first to himself, he collected the people together, in order to sing the poem for them, and solicited my joining with him, which I accordingly did.

As we were singing together, he kept his left arm around my waist, and feeling affected at some passages as he sung them, he would hug and press me up to him; I felt ashamed at such effeminacy, as that of one man to be hugging another; and I must confess, it stretched my modesty to bear with it.—When we had finished singing, the eldest son of the Pastor of the Church (of which the old Gentleman was a member) who was somewhat advance in years, and had a tolerable numerous family, at the same time possessing a tolerable degree of low satirical wit attempted to make me the object of his burlesque, before the people—I immediately broke through all restraint, and lampooned him before the old Gentleman and every person present, without receiving from my old friend the least admonition or rebuke. When the people were gone, I retired with my friend to his house, and asked him how he approved of my performance, he spoke of it in high terms, saying it was exactly agreeable to his will and wishes; no doubt reflecting, that the performance was that of a person, whose conduct and practice, at that time, spoke this language "Depart from me, O Lord! For I desire not the knowledge of thy way." Before I parted with him, he made a second request, which was to this effect—That I would compose him one piece more, with which I complied, and believe I shall have reason to bless God to all eternity for it, its being the means, in the hand of the Spirit, of my awful convictions for sin before God. My old friend also informed me afterwards that he was unusually impressed, that God was about to do something on me or in me, that disposed him to solicit a second composition. When I applied to him to know upon what subject I should make it, he replied he had none to give me, but left it to myself. I felt myself more at a loss what subject to choose, than I was to know his meaning of the word charity, in the first piece.

Leaving his house and crossing the river, which was contiguous thereunto, I had about two miles, through a beautiful and secret place to walk, before I arrived at my school house; and meditating on what subject to select in an instant of time it appeared as if these words were articulate into my heart, and that so forcibly as if another person had spoke them, viz., "Make one on the naturally man's dependence for heaven." An inquiry arose in my breast immediately, what is the natural man's dependence for heaven? Like two contrary voices questioning and answering, the reply was, "What is your own dependence for heaven?" My conclusion immediately presented itself, which was as follows, that sin was so pleasant and agreeable, that I could not part with it, but was determined to pursue the pleasures thereof until I arrived to such an advance in years, that my nature would become dead to the pursuits thereof, and enjoy no further relish for it; at the same time believing that I possessed power by which I could turn to God when I pleased, apprehending also, that God was a merciful God, and that He would accept of a few days or weeks of my sincere repenting, by which my salvation would be secured, my sins pardoned and I received into favour. When this conclusion was drove from me the immediate, reply arose in my mind—this was the natural man's dependence for heaven: not that it was every natural man's dependence, but that a great many natural men had no better foundation than that was. From this conclusion, I immediately set about the performance of my piece. Before I begin it I must make this remark, that the jingle of sound was more the object of my pursuit than the matter contained in it: yet I have often seen since, the overruling hand of Providence in the matter it contained. It is as follows.

1

When I consider, O my God,
How rich men take such pleasure,
Upon this place of earth's abode
Heaping up wealth and treasure,
Not much they'll make
Their souls to stake
T' uphold their pomp and station;
If one them tell
Of heaven or hell
Or the wicked in damnation;
They'll scoff and sneer and ridicule,
Calling such person then a fool,
To tell to them such things as these,
As they won't do but what they please.
Say they we cannot now incline,
To meditate on things divine,
For in our prime,
It is the time
To take our recreation.

2

O! how their consciences they'll bribe,
Under such base pretences,
To gratify their sinful pride,
Committing gross offences;
They'll acquiesce –
There is a bliss
Where righteous men will enter;
Likewise they'll tell
There is a hell,
Where wicked men shall center:
But say they, we're here on earth,

We'll spend our time in Jovial mirth,
And when our youthful pleasure's past
We'll then turn unto God at last;
Few weeks repentance will secure,
Making to us salvation sure,
And save us from
The eternal doom
Of wrath and indignation.

3

But sinners O! whoe'er you are,
Possess'd with such a notion,
That dreadful day will soon appear,
When all things will have motion;
When heaven will roll
Up like a scroll
And vanish with a mighty noise,
And the earth sweat
With fervent heat,
Melting at the great God's voice:
When the archangel will be sent
To raise the dead to judgment,
At God's tribunal to appear,
To answer at His awful bar,
For deeds they've done here on earth,
And their doom pronounced forth;
Either to go
To bliss or woe
And there to dwell for ever.

4

And O! how glorious will prove,
That morning to the righteous;
When with smiling rapturous love
They'll see their Judge Christ Jesus,
With godlike charms,

And open arms
He'll cry—heirs of salvation!
This kingdom too,
Was made for you,
Since the world's foundation;
Therefore with me you shall rejoice,
As you heard and obey'd my voice,
Embrac'd the truths of my gospel,
And oppos'd all the powr's of hell;
Therefore in glory you shall live,
And here a place I will you give,
In heaven's abode
'Long with your God
And the angels forever.

5

But O how dreadful will it be,
When the wicked with terror
The enraged Son of God will see,
Darting forth beams of horror;
Crying depart;
Corrupt in heart,
There's for you no salvation;
For you shall dwell
With fiends in hell
In the regions of damnation;
You spurned at my gospel word,
And abus'd my truth saith the Lord;
Therefore from my presence retire
Into everlasting fire,
Where you with devils there shall roar
And burn in flames for evermore,
And never die,
But gnash and cry,
Through everlasting ages.

6

Therefore O sinners let's embrace,
In order to salvation,
That blessed covenant of grace,
To save us from damnation;
For if we slight
His glorious light,
We're under condemnation;
The law does breathe
Nothing but death,
To slighters of salvation.
Then let our contemplations rise,
And soar on Christ above the skies,
In that celestial abode;
Where Christ is co-equal with God,
Lay hold of Him as scripture saith
Embrace His truths by lively faith,
Then He'll us bring
Where we shall reign
Along with Him in glory.

Book 2

Chapter 1

These words in the author's second composition, were the means of bringing a lasting conviction upon him, viz. "The law does breathe nothing but death, to slighters of salvation." They kept running in his mind, and nothing could disengage his mind from them—He dances once more in company, though none join in the exercise with him—He attends a little meeting and visits a Presbyterian family.

So soon as I had finished this poem, these words in the last verse viz. "The law does breathe nothing but death to slighters of salvation," kept continually running through my mind—Whatever I was engaged in, whether by myself or in company, or singing songs, the above words were continually sounding loudest in my mind, which I could not help taking great notice of, but so wicked, seared and senseless was I, that I could assign no reason for it. It had continued about a day and a half with me, when I went to present my piece of poetry to my old friend; and from the confidence I reposed in him concluded I would state the circumstance to him.

It was Saturday in the forenoon when I visited him; when I presented my verses to him, he read them over and over very seriously; after pausing a little he looked solemnly and steadfastly in my countenance and repeated no other words but these, viz. "O! Man." I concluded I would tell him of these words continually sounding in my mind which I could not get clear of; I then addressed him in the following manner: "Friend, ever since I made this piece these words, 'The law does breathe nothing but death to slighters of salvation,' keeps continually ringing through my mind, neither company nor conversation can banish them from me, leaving always the last impression there. Can you assign any reason why it is so?" He fixed his eyes right on mine for a short time, then bowing his head, I observed him smile—He apprehended, he said, the Lord was about to do something on me, which he afterwards explained. I put a wrong construction on his smile, and concluded he smiled at my extreme weakness, that I have a concern upon my mind at the repetition of a few of the words occurring—so mortified was I that the Devil and passion took possession of my heart, and I felt extremely unhappy in his company. I endeavoured to guard my countenance from being perceived by him, and parted with him under the outward show of our former friendship, resolving when I crossed the river that I would use other exertions than what I ever had done, and drive that foolish notion (as I took it to be) out of my mind.

When I had got at a proper distance so as not be heard, I began to sing wicked and lascivious songs, of which I had a great number; but although I exerted my voice to its utmost power and highest pitch still the words—"The law does breathe nothing but death to slighters of salvation," sounded louder in my mind than the audible exertion of my voice; I would then form my body in to a bending position and putting a hand upon each knee, would exert all the force of nature within me, shake my head and endeavour to force other objects and subjects upon my mind, but nothing could avail to dispossess me of that impression; I therefore, gave over the attempt. Having had an appointment to attend a dance that evening at a certain Gentleman's house, where a number of both sexes met for that purpose; but the dancing that evening was dropped, and I was the only person that exhibited on the floor without the least apprehension of guilt or remorse of conscience. I inadvertently (and yet it appeared to me it was what I could not help) informed the company that I expected that was the last time I should ever dance amongst them! Had they inquired of me the reason of my saying so, I could not have given a satisfactory one. They appeared to look strangely at my expressing myself in such a manner: and if I felt any thing at all, it was some small degree of confusion, the reason for which I could not account. The night having passed over, and the next day being the Lord's Day, there happened to be a couple of young men who came from below the ridge to live with their elder brother; they came of a family or respectability, and it was reported in the neighbourhood that these young men believed themselves converted. A few of the neighbours would convene there on the Lord's Day, with whom they would sing, read the scripture, and speak a little upon what they called their experiences. I concluded to pay them a visit on that day, being the first time.

The passage so frequently mentioned that passed through my mind, was no ways abated. I sat in a serious and pensive manner, and paid much attention to what they said, although they were exceedingly weak in discoursing upon any passage of scripture, which I the more easily discovered after the people retired by a little religious conversation they entered upon with myself. My speculative ideas of doctrines enabled me to support the subject we were upon which, from first to last, was conducted in a manner exceeding friendly. One of them, at parting, imprudently told me, after giving me some wholesome advice, that I possessed the five talents. The encomium did not take place so as to exalt me by the compliment.

A strange confusion was gaining fast upon me, and God was about bringing that to a crisis by which I was both made to see and feel my guilty state. I was going that evening to visit a respectable Presbyterian family, of which the old lady I believe possessed the grace and spirit of Jesus Christ; she had attended at the same place that I had, and was on her return home. On my way to her house, (which was a little better than a mile) I felt an unusual conflict within; the aforementioned words running through my mind, all at once I was made as it were to stand!—God was pleased to manifest light to my understanding, and brought it home to my conscience that I was the slighter and contemner of the salvation of Christ; and that the law of God was then breathing death against my soul. The impression was so forcibly brought home to my conscience, that it never become obliterated from that period until I had reason to believe that Christ was formed in my soul the hope of Glory. When I arrived at the house of my friend and had dined, I felt in such a state of confusion that I concluded I would retire to a secret place and pray to God. I found it was customary for the lady of the house to retire for such a practice; she had been out before me, and discovered the place I retired to, and the duty I went about; and I can venture to say this was the first time that ever I bowed my wicked knees and lifted up my guilty hands under a conscious sense of guilt before God, in all the course of my life. When I returned from the place, the old lady retired to the same time from where she was; we met in a path in the middle of the meadow, which lead to the house and no doubt discovering my confusion, she addressed me seriously in these words, "May every one of us be engaged for ourselves, and may God be for us all."

Chapter 2

The author gives an account of having joined the Freemason brethren, about twelve months before his convictions, and how determined himself and another of them were, never to become Baptists, and how hard they swore that they never would—He returns to his narrative—his convictions increase, in consequence of which he forms new plans and resolutions, and works hard for religion; meanwhile a text of scripture was presented to his mind which gave him some encouragement.

There are a few remarks which I feel disposed to make, and which, perhaps, may not be thought unworthy of being inserted in this narrative, which the introduction to my first religious impressions prevented me from inserting, not wishing to break the line of what I was then upon. They are as follows. Probably it might have been nearly twelve months anterior to my convictions, that I was earnestly solicited by some of my most intimate acquaintants to join with them in a society of which they were members; they distinguished themselves by the appellation of Brethren! Bold and wild as I then was, I sustained many strange conflicts in my mind before I gave up and consented to join them. After joining them and attending many meetings amongst them, I was esteemed an excellent proficient, and soon passed through several grades of advancement; being much enamoured therewith, and the order that was observed in that society, gave me to enjoy amongst them, a considerable degree of pleasure.

I have no object in view, in making any remarks respecting them, further than to observe how wonderfully the Lord was pleased to work upon and amongst these members, a short relation of which will be given in the sequel of my narrative. By referring a few pages back, to my composition upon charity, it will be seen that I gave some hints of attending a Regular Baptist yearly meeting, and how they would address each other by the affectionate appellation of Brethren. Receiving information of the imprisonment of some of the Baptist teachers, and hearing certain false reports that were propagated against them, by the enemies of real and vital religion, I entertained the most violent prejudices against them and their followers. Such was the wickedness and enmity of my heart that I felt myself possessed with a considerable share of the spirit of Saul of Tarsus, who breathed nothing less than threatenings and slaughter against the disciples of the Lord.

I attended one evening at a meeting of that religious society, for whom I had a very singular esteem. After worship was over we retired by ourselves; he asked me what I thought of them? To the best of my remembrance I retorted the question upon him, whose judgment was no way respectful in their favour. He took me by the hand calling me at the same time Brother, and using the appellation by which our society was distinguished, declared himself to this effect—"We will stick to our own profession;" and imprecated the most awful oath that he would never become a Baptist. So hardened was I that in return, I called upon God the Father, Son and Holy Ghost that I never would become one either. This remark I think proper to make because that same person, with myself, in a very short period after, were the two first persons in that settlement (as far as we knew) that were under awful impressions of our guilty states before God. As to other remarks they will transpire in their proper place.

To return to that period of my being awakened to a sense of my guilty state, I feel myself at a loss in a measure to find language to convey a regular series of ideas of that complicated confusion and distress that I felt for two or three days. This I perfectly remember, that those ways and practices which I with so much greediness pursued, and which constituted my leading darling idols, were slain in me at once; neither can I recollect that ever my mind has been pestered with them since.

Restless and uneasy in my mind, I began to plan a mode for myself to pursue; I considered God was offended with me, His law I had broken, and a life of daring impiety I had led in His sight; I concluded to pursue the following plan, viz. that I would endeavour to conform my actions to the law of God; wherever I found I had broken any of the commands, I would confess with sorrow, and hope by praying and repenting, God would be satisfied. I would reform my life by quitting company and conversation with my wicked companions; I would avoid the courses that I had pursued, and become a praying person, or at least, say over some prayers daily to God, thinking that God was all a compound of mercy, without any consideration of His justice, and He would peradventure at last, save my soul. This being a plan of my own projecting, and resolving to execute the same, I avoided the company of the dissipated acquaintances, and to work I went. If heaven could have been obtained by the exercise of human endeavours and self-sufficiency I, perhaps, might have laid in for a claim. From the fears of hell and the terrors of a damned state, and from the light I had then imparted to me, and feeling some degree of the worth of my soul, I laboured hard. And although much enveloped in spiritual darkness yet in duty I was very diligent; and although my whole superstructure was founded upon no other basis than self-merit, I would not have it to be thought, that by the aforesaid remark, I have the least intention to decry an awakened sinner's being solicitously engaged in duty before God for mercy to his perishing soul.

My whole life, as well as the doctrines I have preached, is a manifest indication of the propriety of the same.

I believe it is the duty of an awakened sinner to lay as close siege to the kingdom of heaven, and to storm it with his groans and tears (if I may be allowed this expression) as if he was to merit heaven by the same; at the same time, I absolutely decry putting them in the room of Christ, and making saviours of them; because it would be no less than robbing Christ of His glory, and plucking the brightest pearls out of His mediatorial crown, and lessening His dignity, by attributing that to the creature that is the royal prerogative of the adorable Redeemer. It would be destroying the efficacy of His satisfaction, the meritoriousness of His righteousness, and the influences of His Spirit and grace, in renewing and sanctifying the soul. Although it is the experience of many to linger long under conviction, yet, where God has begun the good work in the soul, He has declared it shall be carried on until the day of Jesus Christ.

Passing by this remark, when under the exercise of the above duties, I was walking in a place of retirement, in a very solitary frame, when that passage of scripture, Isaiah 65:1 bolted in upon my mind, "I am found of them that sought me not." Surprised as I was at the impression it made, I was not certain whether it was scripture or not, until I searched and found it recovered in the above cited place. By this passage, I was led back to see the methods God had first taken to impress my mind, when I composed the pieces solicited by N. F. It was his favour, approbation and applause as well as my own praise that I sought after; yet the Lord shewed me, that although I sought not after His favour or approbation in it, He made that circumstance the very means in the hands of His Spirit, to awaken me to that sense of my state and condition, so far as I had then attained. It was productive of a little contrition, and gave me a distant but feint hope, that God might at last be propitious to me. But alas! My views were then very short to what they came afterwards to be. I had only a discovery of outside or outbreaking sins against the law of God. It pleased God to give me something of the discovery of my innate or inbred corruptions of heart, and that it was from thence my outbreaking practices flowed.

I was then led to see, in some measure, that the law was spiritual and reached even to the discovery of my inbred pollution. When I would read the scriptures I was perfectly satisfied of their being the word of God, more especially the threatenings of the law against the wicked, and in a pointed manner against my soul; they came home with such authority as bore evidence to me of their divine authority and origin. All my former plan for mercy to my soul, was broke and unhinged; the legal spirit had such a possession of my soul, with the wretched and unhappy situation I found myself in, as soon led me to adopt another plan which was as follows. I concluded I would pursue the duties of sorrow, praying and repenting, and perform and do every thing that lay in my power; and concluded that in its place, so far might I be accepted of God; on the other hand, that as the Lord Jesus Christ had suffered and died for sins, and by His death and resurrection had obtained redemption for lost sinners, I concluded that what I could not do, Christ by what He has done would make up the deficiency, which I hope God would accept of. Here was I making a compound between the merits and righteousness of

Christ, and my own works and sincere endeavours; although at the same time willing to give Him the compliment of all.

Being much beloved by my former wicked companions, every artifice in them was employed to get me back to my old courses; but it could not avail; the arrows of conviction were shot deep, by the hand of God, into my soul, so that no attempt of theirs could extract them. I was then almost continually in solitude and retirement, in the woods, imploring the great God for mercy to my soul; and became there in a tolerable degree acquainted with the temptations of Satan, and of the variety of methods he would suggest to my soul, to excite in me at some times a presumptuous hope or split me on the rock of despair of ever God's looking in mercy on such a poor polluted wretch as I felt myself to be.

Chapter 3

The author is tempted to take to himself an earthly companion for life, to which he thought he had consented and consequently had sold Christ, to whom he had frequently prayed to the Father, that he might be wedded. Two of his late companions in sin, who had now apparently, set out in the way of Godliness, turn their backs upon him and become apostates. Nature must have sunk under his trials, had not the Lord supported him by a promise.

I underwent a singular temptation about this time, which I have hesitated at times whether I should insert or not, from an apprehension that some might attribute it to weakness and enthusiastic notions but as I underwent severe conflicts under it, and the whole of the circumstance being matter of fact, I have concluded to venture it. It will lead me back a number of months prior to my awakened state. A person in the parts where I resided, was married to a minister's daughter in Maryland, and whose father was also a minister, both of the Baptist persuasion, although themselves were of a humorous and facitious disposition and conversation. I frequented their house often, where we spent many lively hours together. He would at certain times, undertake to teach vocal music, being well acquainted with the rules and grounds thereof.

At the time that I refer to, one of his schools was about twenty-two miles from his residence; he taught at the house of one Col. Pugh, where he had a numerous school, the quarter part being females. After he had attended them a few times, he solicited me to bear him company there, saying he had a particular reason for it. I asked his reason in confidence; to which he replied, that he always possessed a singular esteem for me, and wished to see me comfortably united with some agreeable female; that there were a number at his school, and there was one among that number who had the preeminence over the rest. He described her in such a manner, as excited some small degree of curiosity in me to see her, although at the same time, nothing was more remote from me than the idea of abridging my liberty, and entering into a state of wedlock; however to gratify him, I consented to go with him; at the same time he told me, she was a daughter in a respectable family, that her father was a man of circumstance, and had no doubt but a match might take place, provided she suited my turn and fancy. I attended him to his school, and after singing a number of tunes an intermission was given; during the intermission I introduced myself amongst the young ladies. The conversation that passed at that time, was what might be called sprightly and innocent. We tarried for two days and then returned homewards, without feeling the smallest impression upon my mind respecting her.

At the time of the distress of mind, I have last recited, not having yet resigned up my school, which I did shortly after, my friend came over to my school house on a visit, and informed me if I would accept of a scholar, there was one coming to board at his house in order to come to school to me. Her boarding at his house was in consequence of the great distance the person would be from home. I inquired who the person was; he immediately replied, it was the young lady that he had invited me to go down to visit; and that she wished to enjoy the benefit of my tuition for three months. However, I had company very soon for the grand adversary of man, Satan, immediately laid siege to my soul; and like unto his once presenting the kingdoms of this world and their glory in a moment of time, to our blessed Saviour, with a promise of bestowing them on Him if He would fall down and worship him; so, likewise, he represented to my imagination, many pleasing prospects and advantages that would result from that viz. taking up with earthly objects, if I would but consent thereto. I was conscious at that time, that these were the suggestions of Satan; so deep were the distresses of my soul, that no human object could ever attract my desire that way. I resisted the temptation, prayed to God to be delivered from it, and exercised the utmost exertions of all my natural abilities, in order to shake the remotest thought of it out of mind. Under the exercise of this struggle, and his violent temptations, a thought seemed to pass through my mind, as if I had consented or said I would.

As soon as this thought passed, it appeared to me that I had sold the Lord Jesus Christ, (though I had been engaged with God, that my poor guilty soul might be wedded to Jesus Christ), that I had set Him at naught and rejected Him, whilst my mind consented to accept of a carnal object in preference to Him. I compared myself then to a bird flying, that had both its wings shot off and dropped to the ground. It is impossible to describe the distress I then fell into from this temptation. I have an hundred times since thought that if ever a creature felt the horrors of despair I then did. So full of confusion was I, that I could not look up to heaven; I conceived that God frowned upon me, and that Christ and all heaven did the same. Repeatedly as I would retire to the woods in prayer to God, I had not a word to say, but like the publican smote upon my breast saying, "God be merciful to me a sinner."

Two or three of my companions by this time appeared to be in some measure engaged about their salvation, and met with me at my school house to spend the night in prayer together. It was at the same period I was under this distress. My lamentable bemoaning my state in their presence, together with the visible anxiety of soul they saw me in, disposed them to turn their backs upon what they were seeking after; and I can say with propriety, they walked with me no more, each returning like the "Dog to his vomit and the sow to her wallowing in the mire." It appeared that nature must have sunk under this trial, had not the Lord been pleased graciously to relieve me from it. Being often retired in the woods, in prayer that God would relieve me and not cast me out from His presence, these words, Hebrews 13:5, last clause, "I will never leave thee nor forsake thee," bolted into my heart, as if an audible voice had spoken them to my ears. My distress as to the temptation was removed, and some small encouragement, and a secret hope arose, by which I was encouraged to seek the Lord, but yet found no basis for the security of my soul to rest upon.

Chapter 4

His friend and countryman hearing of his distress, and that he was going to get converted, boastingly swore he would convert him to the next dance, and goes to accomplish his design; but finding him at his school house in such an altered condition, he is also taken under conviction, which ended in his conversion—More enlarged views of the spirituality of God's law are given him.

It comes now into my way to make some remarks about a man whom I referred to some pages back, and from whom I expected to receive some information relative to my parents and relations. Although a friendship existed between his father's family and my father's family, yet he never was an associate and companion of mine, by reason of the disparity of years between us; yet upon the remembrance of past family acquaintance from the instant of seeing each other, we conceived and preserved a singular affection for each other. He was a member of that fraternity to which I hinted before, I had joined; and was very instrumental in persuading me thereunto; he at the same time possessing the highest place in that society. The news of my awakening impressions, had diffused itself through every part of the settlement and its vicinity. It became the topic in all companies that "James Ireland was going to be mighty good now, for he is going to get converted."

My acquaintance had not seen me for some short period, previous to my soul's distresses. There was a dance appointed to be held the Monday following, at a wealthy neighbour's house. My countryman in company with others, hearing the remarks they were making about me, and being tolerably dissipated in language at times, swore they need not believe anything about it, for there could not be a dance in the settlement without my being there, and if they would leave it to him, he would convert me, and that to the dance, on Monday; and they would see me lead the ball that day. The deep impressions upon my soul had a very considerable influence upon my exterior appearance of body; that wild vivacity that flashed in my eyes, and natural cheerfulness that appeared in my countenance was entirely gone; my eyes appeared solemn and heavy, my flesh began to pine away, my ruddy checks and countenance had vanished, and all that remained was a solemn gloomy paleness, whilst my head was often hanging down like a bulrush, under the internal pressure of my guilty state. This my friend, who had bound himself under an oath that he would convert me to the ball, had never yet seen. Determined however to prosecute his purpose, which I had also been informed of, disposed me to expect a visit from him, in which he did not deceive me. He came to my school house; being there myself, I heard the noise of a creature's feet some little distance from me, which disposed me to look about, and soon I descryed the rider to be my friend, coming to see me. Being fully persuaded he would use all the influence he was master of, to persuade me to his wishes, I was seized with a momentary panic, which disposed me to lift up my heart to the Lord, and implore him not to suffer any reasonings he could use to have the least influence upon my mind, as also that the Lord would direct some word or other, that might be for his benefit.

When I viewed him riding up, I never beheld such a display of pride in any man, before or since, as I beheld in him at that juncture, arising from his deportment, attitude and jesture; he rode a lofty elegant horse, and exhibited all the affectation possible, whilst his countenance appeared to me as bold and daring as Satan himself, and with a commanding authority called upon me, if I were there to come out, which I accordingly did, with a fearful and timorous heart. But O! How quickly can God level pride to the ground, if He does but once touch the heart, as was soon manifested in him. In a few minutes did the person, who, no doubt, made sure, as he came to visit me, of making an easy conquest of me, find that the race is not to the swift nor the battle to the strong. For no sooner did he behold my disconsolate looks, emaciated countenance and solemn aspect, than he instantly appeared, as if he was riveted to the beast he rode on; his passions were so powerfully impressed, that I conceived he would have fainted and dropped from his horse.

For some short space of time, he was past utterance, and did nothing but stare at me with wild amazement. As soon as he could articulate a little his eyes fixed upon me, and his first address was this; "In the name of the Lord, what is the matter with you?" To which I replied, if he would light, hitch his horse, and come into the house, I would tell him. I stepped into the house before him, begging of the Lord to direct my speech unto him; his surprise and consternation still attending him, he repeated his former expression; "In the name of the Lord what is the matter with you?" I instantly took him by the hand, and with a tender heart, and tears streaming from my eyes, spoke to him as follows. "My dear friend I possess a soul that will be either happy or miserable in the world to come; and God has been pleased to give me a view of the worth of my soul, as also of the guilty and condemned state it lies in by reason of sin; and I plainly see that if my soul is not converted, regenerated and born again, I will be damned." Holding my hand fast in his, and looking at me, with all the eagerness of desire, he burst out into the following words, "O! You will not leave me nor forsake me now." To which I answered that I would not, upon condition he would renounce his former wicked ways, as I had done, and seek God through Jesus Christ, for pardon and salvation to our poor souls. To which he replied, with streaming eyes, from that moment forward, through the strength of the Lord Jesus Christ, he would. His convictions were formed that very instant; and from my knowledge of him, meeting often by appointment to pray together to God for the salvation of our souls, I am satisfied that his impressions never subsided until he came to a well grounded hope of an interest in the salvation of God, through the merits of the precious Redeemer; of which I shall have some occasion to speak in the sequel. From this lengthy digression respecting him, I shall now return to the thread of my narrative.

In the preceding pages I have given some account of the views I had of the depravity of my nature, and of the spirituality of God's divine law, and the compound I was making with the merits and righteousness of Christ and my own works—willing to compliment Christ with the whole credit and honour of my salvation, provided I could be a part

Saviour therein. This legal, Pharisaical, self-righteous spirit needed a deeper stroke from the Spirit of Christ, to bring me off of this foundation; and it soon pleased God to bring that about. God was pleased to banish in a great measure, that darkness that pervaded my understanding and give fuller views and discoveries of my original guilt and actual pollution; so that I beheld myself to be a mass and sink of sin; I beheld myself as one that was shapen in sin and brought forth in iniquity, that my heart was corrupt and depraved, deceitful and wretchedly wicked above all things; that the Ethiopian could as soon change his colour, and the leopard his spots, as for me to perform any good action of myself, in the state I then was, or to lay any obligation upon God to bestow His eternal favour upon me. I saw that my iniquities had justly separated between God and me, and that my guilt stood as a bar between God and my soul—I had more enlarged openings of the spirituality of the divine law than ever I possessed before; that it had a power to condemn but not to save, and that salvation was not by the law in part or in whole; for by the deeds of the law no living flesh could be justified. The commandment then came home with effect upon my conscience; sin revived and I died, as to the remotest expectation of my soul's being benefited thereby. I discovered God to be a just God, I possessed a principle in my conscience, that if God had cut the thread of my life, and sent me to hell, I must have said, He dealt justly and righteously by me. O! How precious and how valuable did the worth of my poor lost soul appear to me; had I possessed ten thousand worlds all at my disposal, there would not have been the least hesitation in me, to give them all in exchange for one small ray of hope of Christ's pardoning mercy to my guilty spirit. Language would fail me were I to attempt to give a full description of my temptations and trials then; of the distressing days and sorrowful nights that passed over me; neither do I conceive that any person can form a judgment of these things, excepting such as God hath been pleased, by His Spirit, to convince of sin, righteousness, and judgment; for as the scripture saith, "A wounded spirit who can bear it?"

Chapter 5

The author finds it hard to believe—loathes himself in his own sight, on account of his sins—longs to be made holy—He is sorely tempted by Satan, to believe God had given him up to a hard heart and a reprobate mind—He is established in the doctrine of God's electing love in Christ, and of grace being given to the elect in Him, before the world began.—God applies to him, for his comfort, at the moment of a severe temptation, this scripture, "I will have mercy on whom I will have mercy," Rom. 9:15. Upon this Satan withdraws from him, as if ashamed.

The law coming home with efficacy upon my conscience, and viewing my own plans all cut off, I began to have some view of the Lord Jesus, in a more enlarged light, than I had attained before. I was led to see and feel that he must be a whole Saviour or none, that He was the way the truth and the life (viz.) the way to God the Father, the truth that must be believed in and embraced, and the Possessor of that spiritual life, I must be made partaker of, if ever I am saved. But how to attain to this, I found not. I would hear of other persons talking about faith and believing, and often read in the scriptures that faith and salvation were connected together; however easy it appears to others to believe, it was not so with me; for a poor sinner, enveloped in darkness, and loaded with guilt and sin, to go out of himself and all dependence there, and venture upon an unseen Christ, for eternal happiness, was a work and act beyond myself to accomplish. Thousands were the discouragements that Satan would roll in my way, together with the assiduous endeavours of my old companions to draw me back to my old ways, which disposed me generally to spend the day in the woods.

I viewed myself to be the most wretched, the most wicked, and the most guilty sinner, that existed on the globe. My state appeared so wretched to me that I often thought, if my sin and guilt were imputed to ten thousand worlds, it must have sunk them all under the vengeance and displeasure of God. So vile I felt in my own sight that had strangers to religion accidentally come upon me, at such times, when in the woods, and beheld me dropping upon my knees, wringing my hands, and imploring forgiveness from God, through a Redeemer to my soul; had they heard me mourning like a dove, and chattering like a swallow, they would have conceived me to be a person bereaved of his senses, (which thoughts some entertained at last concerning me) my poor soul being thus pursued by law and justice, and the threatenings of God. O! With what earnestness would my mind be running after Christ, the great city of refuge. But alas! As yet, I could not reach the place.

I observed an alteration with regard of sin. Formerly I would seem to flee from it as from the face of a serpent, but now I could take a view of it, loathe it and hate it in my heart, and myself for it; so that I can say, I felt a fulfillment of what the prophet saith, "Then shall you look upon your ways that were not good, and shall loathe yourselves in your own sight, because of your iniquities and abominations." Such views of the beauty and excellency of holiness I had, as made it appear most amiable and desirable to me. When I would take a view of the excellency of God, the amiableness of His perfections, more especially that of His holiness, which desposed Him to hate sin; and contrasted it with my present state, it excited in me the warmest desires after holiness, and the possession thereof whereby I might never sin, against so just, so pure and so holy a God.

Often was I made to wonder, that God could suffer such a sinner to walk the earth, and not cause it to open its mouth and destroy me, Korah, Dathan, and Abiram like. Often was I melted down under a sense of the goodness of God and His sparing mercy, who still preserved me, when He might in justice have cut me off, and sent me to hell. One resolution was riveted in my heart, which I was determined through the Lord's strength to pursue. If I returned to sin, I saw I would perish eternally; at the same time I found it impracticable for me to do it, because I loathed sin and hated all its ways; but resolved as long as I

lived, I would endeavour to seek the Lord for mercy; and if I perished, I
saw it would be just, and that it should be said in hell at last, "Here went
a soul to hell praying for pardoning mercy." O! How amiable, how
desirable, and how safe, did I behold those whom I conceived were in
the ark of safety: how high they walked with God, and with what sweet
consolation they passed on their pilgrimage. But alas! alas! thought I,
this is not for me, nor never will be.

I still possessed a speculative idea of the doctrine of election,
although according to my past exercises which I have related, being
naturally a legalist, plainly contradicted it. However, at this period, I
went under a solemn and distressing temptation about it. At times I
could feel what is called a soft and broken heart for sin; I would mourn
because I thought I did not mourn enough; I would grieve because I
could not grieve, but all those sensations, at this juncture, seemed to
become extinct in me. I was overwhelmed with such a degree of
hardness, as if the whole moisture of my body was dried up; and for some
weeks I felt, that if I could have commanded heaven, and secured my
eternal peace, by the shedding a few tears, it was not in my power. The
great adversary of mankind took advantage of this, my present situation,
and by his temptations improved it to the distressing sorrow and
disquietude of my soul. He would come in upon me in this
manner—"That it was easy to render a reason for my present hardness,"
and the reason he injected was this—"That I was not elected, that if I
had been elected, God would have given me a soft and broken heart for
sin; whereas on the other hand, I was given over to a hard heart and a
reprobate mind." And as he brought scripture to the dear Redeemer in
his temptations with Him, so would he bring scripture to me, which was
as you may see in Romans 9:18, last clause, "Whom He will He
hardeneth." Then he would apply it in this manner, and request me to
examine my own feelings, and see if I did not carry the marks of
reprobation upon me. I would then examine myself and feel that my
present hardened state, established the temptation, and in a great
measure gave up to the belief of it. My dear reader, if ever thou hast
been under a similar trial thou knowest what such a sore temptation
means. To be lying down and passing lonesome nights, wearisome and
distressing days, under the temptation that I was not within the verge of

God's electing grace in Christ Jesus. Under the influence of this trial I was experimentally established in this point, that there was such a thing as God's electing love in Christ, and of grace being given to such before the world.

It is not my object at present, to enter into any controversial point upon that head of doctrine, because it is unsuitable, as well as inconsistent with my present designs. Some I have blamed, who, perhaps, from an unguarded zeal have publicly attempted the defense of it, who did not possess requisite qualifications to manage it; whilst I have blamed, on the other hand, many who have attempted the reprobation thereof, which has led me to conclude, from the scandalous epithets they would throw out against it, that probably they were unacquainted with the operations of the doctrines of efficacious grace, upon their own hearts. But what I write now, is only my own experience. O! How happy did I conceive those to be who possessed the witness in themselves, of an interest in God's everlasting love. As often as I would retire to pray for the pardon of my sins, the enemy would discourage me by saying it was in vain, still pursuing me with the above passage, "Whom He will He hardeneth."

At length the season of my deliverance arrived. One evening between sun down and dark, I retired to a remote place, about half a mile from my school house, under the greatest conflict I had yet experienced, from my present temptations, which was brought about in this manner; wringing my hands together, I cried out "O! Lord if Thou hast not given me over to a hard heart and reprobate mind; and if Thou hast any purposes of mercy to my poor soul, wilt Thou be pleased to deliver me from this distressing temptation?" At that instant the enemy backed my prayer in this manner, "It is in vain, you are too wicked a sinner, and God has given you over to a hard heart and reprobate mind," for "Whom He will He hardeneth." In a moment it appeared as if a voice from Heaven reached my soul with these words. "But I will have mercy upon whom I will have mercy." I instantly apprehended it came from God, for the relief of my wounded spirit, and I hope it will not be accounted as wild enthusiasm, to say, at that instant, I possessed a certainty of Satan's presence with me, in that temptation, and that he now withdrew from me, as a tempter that was ashamed and conquered.

I did not arrive at any establishment here of the safety and security of my soul in Christ; but it appeared only to me that I had been under the temptations of the devil, and God had applied that passage by way of encouragement, to continue to seek for God's mercy through the Redeemer. The prophet Jeremiah, cried out under the views of God's judgments, impending over his guilty nation—"Oh that my head were waters and my eyes a fountain of tears, that I might weep day and night for the slain of the daughters of my people," (Jeremiah 9:1). At that time I had not this to wish for, relative to myself; the great deep of the barren fountain of my heart, was then broke up, my head I could then say, was like to a well of water, whilst the tears from the two fountains of my eyes ran down for several hours, without intermission; and of all the tears that ever I shed in my life, these were the sweetest and the most delectable. My hard heart was thawed into contrition, whilst my soul lay low in the dust before God, under the sweet impressions of His present goodness, deliverance and encouragement to me. I left my school house under a deep conflict, but returned back again with a soft and broken heart for sin.

Chapter 6

A singular instance of the power of an enlightened conscience, when acting for itself, against one who had committed sin. Our author, by this time, had become dead to the allurements of worldly prosperity; his townsman gets converted, but himself is again left to the temptations of Satan for a season.

By this time awakening impressions began to take place in others; and a singular circumstance transpired worthy of remark, as it will tend to show the efficacious power of divine grace, upon the heart, when once it is touched thereby. I only aim to illustrate the power of divine grace, without ever mentioning the name of person, family, or connection; the whole is as follows, viz. About twelve months before the present date (sometime in 1768 or 1769) there were two persons, who loved their glass very well, agreed to meet at a certain house to spend the evening and enjoy themselves. As I was informed they had drank pretty freely together, and perhaps had got to that pitch, that they were incapable of judging of an action, whether right or wrong. The man of the house being a plain unsuspicious person, came into the room where they were, lifted up the lid of an open chest, put into the till thereof, a half joe, and two dollars, shut the lid down and so went out. One of these two persons discovering that the man of the house deposited something there, got up, and went to the chest, lifted up the lid, and took out the money.

If I can recollect my information, the landlord found it out before they left the house. I can tell no more of the circumstances at that time, only I was informed afterwards, that the loser of the money applied to a magistrate, and had the suspected person brought before him. The fact could not be established upon the guilty person, and he was therefore acquitted without his character suffering by it. This very person got under awakening impressions about twelve months afterwards; he had kept the money without expending it, and his convictions worked so powerfully upon his heart, especially the circumstance relative to the money, that he came to me when under my distresses and opened his own particular case; that with regard to the money, he said it lay very heavy upon his conscience; I replied shortly and briefly to him—That if he had no other sin against him but that one, it would damn his soul. In great anxiety, he asked me what he should do in this matter? I told him to make restitution; for that he could never expect God would pardon his sins if he, Achan like, would conceal the injustice he had done. He went off to the man, who was the proprietor of the money, desired him to walk a little with him towards his stable, and thus addressed him. "You remember, Sir, that at such a period you lost such a sum of money." That is very true replied the man—"You also judged me for it, and by warrant brought me before a magistrate on account of it"—I did he replied—"You remember also you could establish nothing against me, that could injure my character"—It was so, said the man.

The aggressor immediately replied, "I did take your money, and still have it in possession, except a small part, which I will make up to you. The hand of man could not find me out, but the hand of God hath reached me, and I believe I should assuredly go to hell, were I to conceal this act of injustice from you." With that the aggressor dropped upon his knees, saying the pride of my heart, for the sake of my reputation, would have led me to conceal it; so you need not thank me but God, whose almighty power hath touched me. With that he lifted up his hands towards heaven and implored God for pardon to his soul on account of it; then looked the man in the face, and begged for his forgiveness and pardon also. If my information be correct, in what follows it was this; the man was so struck with the candour and honesty of the other, and with what God did impress him with at that time, that he dropped upon his knees also, imploring God for mercy to both their souls. What lasting effects it produced I will not undertake to say, but can say, after my ministry commenced, I always observed that person to be an attentive hearer of the truths of Jesus.

From this digression, I shall now return back to my own narrative. The great concerns of my soul, rendered me incapable to discharge my duties to the pupils that were put under my tuition; and my conscience would not admit me to accept of a compensation, from my employers; under those circumstances I therefore resigned up my school. I had obtained the loan of a bed for my use, which I kept at the school house, and that for this reason: my old companions never desisted from using all possible endeavours to lead me back to sin, and made it a point with them to inquire where I was to be on such and such nights, in order to be there to pursue their designs. Having a bed at my school house, I could, at their approach immediately withdraw myself into the woods and avoid their perplexities; where my time was spent, constantly engaged with God, that He would pardon my sins, for Christ's sake.

Many lonesome and distressing days and nights passed over me, under the pressures of a hard heart and a wounded spirit, without possessing much further discoveries, than what I had for some time past experienced. So mortified and so dead to the things of this world were I, and my whole soul so swallowed up after one thing needful, that at those times I would contemplate this idea; that if a person was sent to me, with certain information, that a rich estate had fallen to me, as apportion, by which I could now live in affluence and swim in flowing tides of sensuality and pleasure; that, when these circumstances were relating, I should have taken my hand and put it upon the mouth of the relater. So completely dead I felt myself with respect to worldly prosperity. As I have already given a relation of the application of the law to my conscience, of its power and spirituality, and that there was no justification before God by the works thereof, as performed by myself. I at this time also, viewed myself to be in a state of spiritual death, and possessed no more power to perform a spiritual action, spiritually good before God than a man literally dead, would be able to see, to hear, to breathe, to feel, and to walk about in his own strength.

I expect my reader recollects my account of the person that first came to the school house, in order to convert me to a dance, and of the impressions at that time formed upon him; that the same person was also my countryman and townsman. I shall now, once more, bring him into view, in consequence of a very singular trial I underwent on his account. He and I had appointed the evening before, to meet at a certain place, an hour before sun down, in order to devote the night together in prayer; the north river of Shenandoah was between us. I stood upon a noal, by the bank of the river, and called aloud upon him several times, but received no answer; then wheeled about in order to return to my school house; and whilst under my disappointment, used the following expression, to wit, "The will of the Lord be done;" at which period he was actually going through the pangs of the newbirth. Next morning he paid me a visit at my school house; when I discovered his countenance, as he rode up, I plainly saw a visible alteration in it. There appeared something of a lightness and a serenity in it, much changed from that solemn aspect he carried in it before. What construction to put upon the change I saw I did not know; but rather embraced the worst, and possessed a fear he had lost his convictions, and was about to use some persuasion with myself. I was instantly seized with such a weakness and tremour over my whole body as became very visible to him. He stepped immediately before me, and in an affectionate manner, begged of me to follow him, and not be afraid; which I immediately did, but with abundance of fear.

When arrived to a private place, he turned about to me, and with the utmost expression of countenance, dropped upon his knees and lifting up his hands and eyes towards heaven, cried out, "I have found the Lord Jesus Christ precious to my soul." I was so overcome that I dropped as if I had been shot, and Satan improved this circumstance to the great distress of my mind, whilst he came home upon me with this scripture, "Two of a city, the one taken the other left." So powerful was the temptation and the circumstance of our both being of one city, a fact which made me give up to it that it was so, I was tempted to believe that the Lord had only formed the impressions He did upon me, that in the course of His providence, He might make use of me, as an instrument, to speak to His case; having had previous purposes of mercy towards Him, and at that time manifested it to Him, whilst I was left behind. I have often thought, respecting this person, that after his conversion he traveled in spirit for my deliverance, with as much engagedness as he was exercised with about himself. But all this could not avail to my comfort. O! The distresses and deep conflicts I underwent at this time. You who are the followers of the blessed Redeemer, and that have ever walked in similar paths with me, know the awful devices of that adversary, who is unwilling to part with a soul, who has once been a faithful servant to him.

Chapter 7

Two passages of scripture are almost successively presented to his view; the first of which gave him great comfort, the second respected faith, and set him on exerting himself to get it; first in his own strength, but he soon saw it was purely the gift of God. Other words were applied to him, which gave him unspeakable comfort. He gets under darkness and gloominess again.

The period was now drawing on when I experienced delivering grace. An account of my general views and exercises at this time will be in a measure, to repeat things I have already said. I possessed a continued conviction that I justly merited hell, being a sinner; that God could not be unjust in sending me there, which I have confessed upon my knees hundreds of times. I saw the consistency of the soul's being saved in and through the Lord Jesus Christ alone. Sometimes it would appear to me that my guilt and pollution like clouds, or mountains, reached up to the heaven's against me; and that I was like a person they had neither hands nor feet, either to walk or climb, yet must get over it, if ever saved. There was a memorable night, which I expect with other things, I will remember to all eternity. It was on a Friday night, at my school house, which I passed under the most awful views of my state possible; some time before day I got into a slumber, but awakening about day break, with my heart lifted up to God, this passage forced itself into my soul, as if God had spoken it from heaven to me—"Thou art of Abraham's seed, and an heir according to the promise," (Galatians 3:29). It was the most heavenly consoling encouragement that ever I had yet experienced, during my sorrows and troubles.

How long I continued under its influence, is not in my power to determine, but I felt for some time, as if my soul was in heaven.

Encouragement I only call it, because on this my soul did not rest. When its sweet influence began, in some measure to subside, that passage in Acts 16:31 was powerfully applied; so far as I relate in the verse, the words were—"Believe on the Lord Jesus Christ, and thou shalt be saved." I was immediately led to view, that nothing separated me from Christ, but the want of faith; that if I only possessed faith, in the blessed Redeemer, I should be saved. I had believed that the legal spirit of yet doing something for my safety was subdued and gone; yet I at this time, found I had a considerable share of it about me. Under the influence of the above scriptures, and their pointed application I arose up out of bed, put on my clothes, went out into the woods a considerable distance, with a full resolution not to return back, until I had believed in Jesus Christ; and this I may venture to assert was the last day, that ever I struggled and worked for justification by the deeds of the law. I considered that faith was an act of the whole soul; and that with the heart man believeth unto righteousness; in which view I conceive I was right, but herein lay my error; I was engaged to produce and perform that act myself.

Through the greatest part of the day, was I painfully and laboriously engaged to force my heart to believe on Jesus Christ, and to throw myself upon Him, so as to derive comfort from Him, and salvation in Him. It would appear almost incredible for me to tell how often I would drop from my feet upon my knees, in order to affect what I went out resolutely determined to perform. At last it pleased God to give me to see, that salvation was by grace through faith, and that not of myself for it was the gift of God, for, as the scripture saith, "Unto you it is given to believe," and that faith by which the soul is saved, must come from God, and be wrought in the heart by the Holy Spirit. Then was I led to cry to God, to grant me that divine faith, which I could not produce in myself. From these views I left my secret retirement, and returned to my school house, in which I spent a very solitary night.

Next day being the Lord's Day, and understanding that a certain minister was to preach, I concluded to go to hear him; concluding at the same time, to pay a visit to my good old friend N. F. that morning before meeting. As I was walking down the main county road by myself, being pretty early, my present sensations according to the best of my

recollection, were as follows—I viewed and felt myself the most odious
and polluted being existing; such was the pressure of my burdened
spirit, that I felt as if the leaders and muscles of my limbs and joints
were incapable to support the weight of my body; I still viewed God as
an unreconciled God to me; I could not say that Jesus was mine, for I
thought all heaven was frowning upon me.

In this situation I descended a short declivity in the road, and when
I arrived at the bottom, in a moment of time, there seemed like a voice
from heaven, that echoed into my soul these words—"O love! O light! O
glory!" I lost all remembrance of being upon earth, and something
appeared to me, although not in a distinct manner, as if I was present
with the happy spirits above. I was upon my feet when the above words
were applied to me, and how I got upon my knees I cannot tell; but
when I came to the exercise of my rational powers, I found myself upon
them. I arose upon my feet, under the deepest impressions of humility
and gratitude to God; all that pressure of sin and guilt that burdened my
soul appeared to be removed and gone; heaven had another aspect and
appearance to me, and so great was the peace and calm diffused through
my soul, that the transition almost seemed too great for nature to bear.

I was then led to view the words that were applied to me, viz. love,
light, and glory; and they opened up to me in this light, so as to
represent faith, and the effects of faith, and the method of salvation
through a Redeemer. The word light, as it came to me, appeared to
represent faith as a ray of light that opened up in my soul, or as the eye
of the soul that looked unto Jesus and discovered a reconciled God in
Him. The word love, appeared an effect of faith at that time; as faith is
said to work by love; and the word glory, represented to me, a glory in
God's method of salvation through a Redeemer, where faith beheld it
and worked by love—I trusted and rested upon it. As I moved along, I
viewed further, that the words that came to me, viz. love, light and
glory, were expressive of the very being, essence and attributes of God.
Other views I had of a reconciled God in Christ, of the righteousness of
the Redeemer, particularly so far as it related to my interest therein,
which I have related in my youthful days to my bosom Christian friends,
yet for want of a perfect remembrance of every circumstance at
present, relative thereto, I shall drop that part of the relation, as

something will come in, in the sequel concerning my exercises that will open up those things.

It was with a burdened soul and heavy heart that I sat off that morning to visit my old friend: but with what pleasing alacrity did I pass along the latter part of the way in order to tell him what I hoped God had done for my soul. O! How we did rejoice together; and it appeared like a new conversion to the good old man's heart. How long I continued with him I cannot say, because such moments are apt to glide sweetly along. The next object that drew my attention was to visit, that evening, the Presbyterian lady, who had been so religious a friend to me. When at her house, I solicited a little retirement with her, and opened up to her God's dealing with me that day. Before I ended my relation, whatever God's design might be in permitting what follows, I know not, but the sweet light of His countenance was instantly withdrawn, and an awful gloom of darkness pervaded my whole soul, whilst a conflict of horrid temptations attended me in the sequel.

Chapter 8

The author prefers being alone—He is tempted to curse each person in the Trinity—Is considered by his old friends and companions in sin, as being a fool, a mad man, and in despair—Composes a poem to that effect.

The sweet consolations I possessed that day, and the awful gloom I experienced next evening, greatly alarmed me, and disposed me to believe, that I had lost my conviction, and the enemy gained an advantage over my soul, as will be shown hereafter. I then again endeavoured to regain my former conviction, and to bring the condemning power of the divine law upon my conscience, the same as I had experienced early that morning; but I found it all in vain. Then I endeavoured to reach forward, if possible, to attain to the enjoyment of that divine peace, and heavenly tranquility I was made to possess through the day, but found this as impracticable as the other. I compared myself to a traveler walking along a beautiful road, who by accident had fallen into a deep and heavy mire up to his ears, but in attempting to return from whence he came, or to proceed forward on the course he wished to go, for the want of a friend to reach out the helping hand to his assistance, he found himself incapable to do either, and therefore must perish.

Such I then believed was my situation. My disconsolate feelings at that time, and the distress that I underwent, made them more oppressive than when under convictions—For when under convictions I possessed a secret hope that probably God might be favourable at last, but that hope seemed almost extinct. Solitude and retirement in the woods, in prayer to God, was my daily practice, and I was divested of all desire of seeing any friends or acquaintance, in order that I might spend my time in solitude, mourning and lamenting about the unhappy state of my soul. During the conflict I am now relating, until the time of my deliverance, I dare not say that I had no encouragement and support under it, for I experienced some in a particular manner, which shall be related in its place.

I have lately said that the enemy gained an advantage over my soul. My meaning was, I fell into a conflict of horrid temptations, which I wish here to be inserted for two reasons—The first is, that they really were so as I relate them—The second, that many of God's dear people, having laboured under similar trials, have concluded it could not be consistent with a state of grace for a person to be tempted thus; and by concealing their trials from experienced Christians, have suffered great perplexities of mind on account of them. To come to my trials—I was tempted to curse God, to curse Christ, and to curse the Holy Ghost—the Trinity in unity and the unity in Trinity—To curse the holy scriptures and every book that had the name of God, of Christ, or of the Holy Spirit in it; and so powerful were these temptations, and so powerful were my efforts in striving against them that my tongue has blistered in my mouth under the fearful apprehension that I should have consented thereto.

My old companions in vanity, were divided in their conduct towards me. When some of them would discover I was meeting them in the road, they would retire into the woods until I passed them, under the apprehension that they would be subjected to admonition or reproof, as I rarely suffered any of them to pass without the one or the other; whilst others of them who possessed some greater degrees of natural affection for me pursued the old line of what they thought was acting for my good. I can say I have been traced by them at considerable distance into my retirements. At such times they would tell me they were sorry for my case they pitied me and declared my senses were all gone. The last person, if I recollect right as to time, if not to circumstance was, as hereafter related, one, who had filled several important stations, such as governor, a general and a member of congress, and with whom I was in habits of intimacy. Whether he came upon me in the woods by any sound of my voice, deploring my unhappy condition or not, is immaterial; but so it was, he came where I was, and

under apparent consternation, addressed me this import—"Jemmy, you
have turned a fool, you are certainly distracted and raving in despair."
What reply I made him at that time I don't recollect; yet so desirous was
I to avoid my teasing acquaintance, that I took up my lodging at a good
old Presbyterian friend's house, whose residence was contiguous to
Massanuttin Mountain; to which mountain I would retire every morning
with my bible and hymn book, and spent a considerable number of days
in said mountain under the anxious concern of my soul. My sense of
guilt appearing to be gone, and the lonesome distresses I then felt,
together with the reflections my companions made drew from me the
following composition, which I addressed to the Lord.

1

Come Lord in mercy 'suage my grief
And from me not depart;
But send some comfort or relief,
To ease my wounded heart.

2

For now my guilty sinful load;
Seems from my heart has di'd;
Therefore let it not go, O God.
From me uncrucifi'd.

3

But let the blood that was in whole
Upon the cross all split,
Be now appli'd to my poor soul,
To cleanse me from my guilt.

4

And likewise Lord, since from my heart;
My sense of guilt seems gone,
I love to be from noise apart
My case for to bemoan.

5

Which makes all those of earthly minds,
Strange stories on me raise;
And also my young carnal friends,
Have turn'd my enemies.

6

For I do but by them walk,
They say I've turn'd a fool;
Then I become their common talk,
In scorn and ridicule.

7

Where'er they see me griev'd or sad,
Walking myself alone;
Poor thing they say, I know he's mad,
His senses are all gone.

8

They say they're sorry for my case,
And likewise will declare,
Telling me plainly to my face
I'm raving in despair.

9

Therefore O Lord, their hearts do smite
With a sore sense of sin;
And make them feel the dreadful state
By nature they are in.

10

That they may know such madness too,
Themselves must also find,
If e'er Thy grace do bring them through,
To holiness inclin'd.

11
Come now O Lord, implant in me
One drop of saving grace;
That I may be conform'd to Thee
In ways of holiness.

12
Then shall my heart and soul both join,
Thy ways for to approve;
And will likewise my sorrows own,
To be Thy chast'ning love.

Whatever poetical compositions are here related, I choose to make them appear in their original dress as I composed them, or there would be no difficulty in making them appear with a better gloss.

Chapter 9

One of the author's young companions threatens to have a chain made for him, and chain him, upon the supposition that he was mad—upon this he handed his friend the last poem he had made, which proved a means of his conviction immediately, and finally of his conversion—He gets into a disconsolate frame, a passage of scripture he opened, gives him a short relief, but that is again taken from him by Satan's temptations.

The greatest torment that ever I experienced by my old companions was from a young man, whose native residence was in Maryland. He loved me to an extreme, and in my distresses would often tell me he must take a final leave of me in about six months: that before he would lose the benefit of my company and conversation for that period, he would forfeit five hundred pounds if he then possessed it. When I had finished the above poetical composition he intended a visit to me, and consequently called at my school house for that purpose. The principal conversation that passed at this time was this; "How is the state of your mind now?" to which I replied, as when he saw me last; he said he was sorry for it; that a young man who was as much thought of as I was, should forfeit all public esteem by becoming a fool—That I had a few friends, himself being the principal one among them, who for former love and respect for me, were determined to take care of me, as he plainly perceived I could not take care of myself; to accomplish which purpose, he called at the black-smith's below me, to get him to make a nice handsome chain with a view to secure me from destroying that existence that perhaps might be restored in future. One thing grieved him, that I had resigned up all that sprightly behaviour which was pleasing to company, lost my senses and become a fool.

After he had finished his remarks I replied to him, since I am deemed a fool by others and yourself here is a piece of poetry I have made, you may take it and read it over, and there behold my folly.—A few of the first verses being expressive of the language he used to me himself, determined me to observe his countenance while he read it. He read it to himself very deliberately, whilst I was engaged in watching him; after he had finished reading it once, he began to read it a second time. I perceived him draw his breath pretty lengthy, from that it would come to a sigh or two, then to a groan. He rose upon his feet with an apparent consternation in his countenance, handed me the piece and said, "I believe that we are all fools, and you are the only wise man amongst us," and then left me. These impressions were formed upon his soul from God at that period, but how or in what manner he related them to me, has escaped my mind; however, he visited me next evening, as he said he could not stay away.

The design of next evening's visit was in order to make me acquainted with what he both saw and felt upon himself, and with a view to contribute to my comfort by the relation he had to give. In the course of our communication together, when our conversation upon the subject ended, I exhorted him to be importunate about the one thing needful; told him how conducive it would be to my satisfaction if he attained unto it; solicited him to favour me with opportunities of his company, in matters of such weighty importance where we might converse and pray together; and if circumstances required it, to give him the best advice I could; not knowing but providence might bless them unto him; and in the judgment of charity, I humbly believe that God was pleased to reveal His Son in him at last the hope of glory. He was the last on in our fraternity there that was brought home to God through Jesus Christ; and it must be acknowledged that God did work very powerfully amongst us.

I observed a few pages past, that after my deliverance, I fell into a conflict of horrid and awful temptations, which attended me on and off for a considerable time. I further observed that I enjoyed some encouragements and supports under them, but through the prevailance of unbelief, they were not abiding. When I would visit my retired places for prayer, time after time, I would feel as if I was overshadowed with the presence and comforts of God; I would continue upon my knees filled with wonder and admiration, desirous of vocally attributing praise to God, while a holy awe would diffuse itself through me, and my tongue would appear as if it clave to the roof of my mouth, incapable of attributing praises to God in a vocal manner. When I would arise upon my feet that heavenly frame would feel to vanish, the sweetness and relish thereof would be gone and unbelief soon creep in. I would then fall into my disconsolate frames again.

Having retired to my school house to spend some time there, wore out and almost exhausted in body and in mind, anxiously engaged with my maker to attain to some degree of certainty whether God had done any thing savingly upon my heart or not. To be free from every apparent incumbrance, and to avoid an opportunity of any of my friends, who might come to see me, I retired a considerable distance from my school house, whilst the sum of my engagements to the Lord was that if He had wrought a gracious change in my soul, He would manifest the same by His word and Spirit to me; but if on the other hand, I had rested short of Christ, He would also be pleased to grant me such indication of the same as would satisfy me on that head, in order that I might pursue such duties as was consistent with the condition of such a poor sinner as I saw myself to be.

It was in this frame I went off from my school house, and in this exercise I was engaged when retired, and returned in the same manner back to my school house. When within a small distance of the house, I was determined in a dependence on God, that when I entered it I would take the Bible and open it, and the first passage my eyes fixed upon I should consider it as directed from the Lord to me. To this end I prayed as I walked in, "O Lord if the work is not completed, but is yet to be done, let the passage I cast my eye upon confirm me of the same: if the work is done, so far as respects my conversion, let the passage confirm me therein." With a heart fixed on God for the issue, I walked about three or four steps, opened the scripture, the words that presented themselves to me are recorded in Revelation 21:6, second clause, which were—"It is done." They came home with such effect upon me (being the express subject of my prayer) that filled me with wonder and astonishment. I found myself upon my knees, but did not know how I got there.

For a short period I was persuaded God spoke to me from that passage; but the conflict I immediately felt, did not suffer me to enjoy any respite, to realize or appreciate the same; so that I have often thought, that never two men who turned out to wrestle in the presence of others, exhibited more active endeavours, in their conflict of manhood together, than Satan and myself did that evening. I think the contest between us continued for about two hours. Myself with my weak and feeble faith, grasping at the words, believing and hanging to them as directed from God to me; whilst my grand adversary, on the other hand, exerted all his devices in order to wrest the words from me and lead me to discredit them. Towards the conclusion of the trial, he would suggest to my mind that there was no rational ground of confidence to be placed upon them, in the way and manner I applied them. I found my confidence gradually shaking and the enemy at length prevailed.

Chapter 10

A minister comes sixty miles to preach to him and his religious associates, and continues two days among them preaching; he could feed on the sermons, which were well adapted to his case, but his faith could not fully apply Christ to his soul as yet; however, not many days afterwards, he received such bright manifestations as enabled him to take up Christ by faith and rest upon him.

About this time a certain minister of Christ, whose services had been signally useful, on hearing of the work of the Lord that had broke out amongst us, upon being applied to, gave us a visit, although he lived sixty miles from there, complied without hesitation. The doctrines he chiefly treated upon, were well adapted to the conditions of us in these parts, at that time; being chiefly on vital and experimental subjects. When he came to attend his meetings, his preaching was at the house of my then residence; he preached two days, and I can say it was the sincere milk of the word to me, so far as this, that nothing scarcely he treated upon, but I possessed an acquaintance therewith in my heart through the general course of my exercises. But still I could not draw this conclusion as to say, "Christ is mine and I am His." The infinite worth and value of my precious soul, determined me not to take a truth upon trust from any man; reject it I must unless the Lord applied it and established it in my heart.

Although not banded together in society, in a regular manner, we yet were banded together in love, and loved as brethren. The brethren, as I may call them, would often endeavour to comfort me, and tell me, "That if ever a work of grace was wrought in the heart of any, it was in me," but I would not give them credit for what they said. The minister took an occasion to solicit some time of retirement with me, and begged of me to take the freedom to give him a relation, from first to last, of the general exercises of my mind, which I honestly and candidly did. In the conclusion he informed me that I ought to be thankful to God, and place my confidence in Him; that in the judgment of charity I was converted, and had experienced a gracious change from God. With a modesty peculiar to myself at that time, I informed him that I was afraid to believe so without some further establishing evidences from God. He gently smiled. We returned to the house and spent the night in agreeable and godly conversation. He left us next morning, in order to attend a meeting at a place called the White House in the Massanutten settlement; at the same time leaving appointments to come and visit us soon again.

What prevented me from going over to hear him, I do not at present remember, but it was something particular. However, my friend that was engaged to convert me to the dance, and my other friend who had applied for a chain for me, both went over with a number of others to hear him. I waited anxiously in the evening for their return; when they came I was very solicitous in inquiring about the sermon, and the effects that attended it; of which they gave me very agreeable accounts. After a comfortable evening's conversation, the time came for those two friends to go home. I walked from the house with them into the bottoms where corn was planted; perhaps it was ten o'clock or a little later; I proposed to them that we could not part until we had united together in prayer severally.

Whilst the person was praying, whose conviction I was perfectly satisfied with, all at once it pleased God to shed abroad His rich love and grace in my heart; I viewed then the glorious Redeemer as my Saviour; my whole soul ran out by faith on Him as such; and my faith was enlarged, and I can say from my heart I believed unto righteousness. I was enabled then to take a retrospect back to that happy time (I have given a relation of) on the great road, and saw that *that* was the time when God converted my soul, removed my burden of sin and guilt, giving me to possess that peace which was beyond understanding. I retired to my lodging, and whilst sitting a short time, I was filled with a second manifestation of His presence; unable to secret it from the view of the family, and desirous to retire humbly to express my thankfulness and gratitude to God for His present mercies and loving kindness to me, I retired. When on my knees out of doors, I was graciously favoured with a third manifestation of God's love, etc. O! The sweet humility of soul I then felt, and how low did I lie in the valley at that time. I returned to the house, and thought that those within appeared with very pleasing countenances, which I appreciated arose from what they informed me of afterwards, I think next day, that they took notice of my exercises, and was satisfied [with] what was the cause of my retirement.

BOOK 3

Chapter 1

The author relates a remarkable dream; gives an account of his entering
upon his ministry; his rapid progress in divine knowledge, etc.

Having now given you a relation of my troubles and sorrows,
encouragements and deliverances, during the months of my distresses
(although I have omitted a variety of particulars on account of my
present, weak state) I shall next proceed to introduce the beginning and
progress of my ministry, which soon took place. But previous to this, I
shall give an account of a most remarkable dream I had, the
accomplishment of which I shortly after saw and experienced in every
circumstance thereof; and were it necessary, I could have the same
established by living witnesses, to whom I immediately communicated
the dream, and who also know how it was accomplished. I shall omit at
present giving my sentiments on dreams in general, which, if I did it
would be seen, that I do not give into the notion of dreams in general
being ominous.

One night I dreamed I was taken prisoner by a man mounted on a
red horse, who carried me over two mountains, there being a
considerable distance between them; when descending the ridges of the
second, he conducted me along edging to the right, about two-fifths of
the whole distance from whence I was taken. I was then led into an old
field, where several buildings were erected on our right, but in none of
them was I to reside. I was conducted some distance into the field, and

deposited in a little old open house, wherein I entered to remain a prisoner until by prayer and supplication, and other necessary methods, I was to be relieved and delivered therefrom.

There were certain circumstances to take place, and duties to be performed before my imprisonment was to take place. I saw I had a lengthy journey to perform, which lay in a southerly direction from that old field; I pursued my journey and arrived at the place intended; but unforeseen obstacles lay in the way, when I got there, which prevented the accomplishment of my purposes at that place. I saw now, that to accomplish my purposes, I had to go a certain distance in a westerly direction, which I accordingly did, and there appeared to me a large house which they called a church; I walked three times round its outside, and then went in at the door.

Immediately after this, I journeyed again, and traveled through beautiful walks, gentle and delectable risings, rocky and cold valleys, sometimes in water and sometimes on land, until I came to a beautiful building above, called my Father's house; And then I awoke. But the impression it made upon my mind was a lasting one, nor could it be eradicated therefrom.

I communicated it to some of my confidential friends immediately; and I often realized upon it, to see what might reasonably be inferred from it. I inferred therefrom, that there were some particular trials awaiting me, that I would be subjected to in the sequel.

It being a persecuting time in our then colony of Virginia, and particularly so against the society with whom I soon after joined. I knew that the man on the red horse, spoken of in Revelation 6:4 denoted persecution; but in what character, I should suffer, I knew not then, though I had the woeful experience of it afterwards, which will be stated in its proper place.

I shall now proceed to the beginning of my ministry—Enjoying a comfortable and established state of mind—with regard to my salvation in the Redeemer, I made, in a little time, a very rapid progress in experimental and divine knowledge: I call it a little time, for it was not many weeks. You will recollect, that the minister who had visited us some time past, had left appointments to be with us soon again; he was to have been up on a Saturday evening, in order to preach on the Lord's

Day, and then to give us what further time he could spare. When the time came, he did not appear, and as the principal body of those who were lately converted, met at our friend's house that evening, in order to give him a welcome reception, his not coming filled us with a degree of despondency, and more especially as he did not come at all. Some unforeseen circumstance must have prevented his coming, as he was generally punctual to his appointments.

It is customary to observe, that whatever a person loves he desires, and what he desires he feels anxious about until he knows whether he is to enjoy it or not. This was our case at that time—We loved to hear the preacher, therefore, was anxious to see him amongst us. Our hopes had not become extinct from the supposition that he might have lodged on the other side of the Massanutten Mountain. If disappointment, at this time, was to be our lot, we were looking about among ourselves, who should go forward that day to speak a word in the name of the Lord. As the day began to advance, and people began to come in, our hopes of the minister's being there vanished.

We retired to confer among ourselves who should go forward, and the result was, it was fixed on me. It was expected but little would be said; but the people were very ignorant and seemed desirous that a few words of exhortation should be given by some of us.

Under a consciousness of the greatness of our undertaking, some of us retired to a private place and there poured out our hearts to God for His presence, aid and assistance.

About twelve o'clock, a tolerably large congregation were met. In dependence upon God, and in fear and much trembling, I went forward. Worship was introduced by singing the 12th or 15th Hymn according to Doct. Watts. It begins thus—"Let me but hear my Saviour say." The hymn was expressive of the real exercise of my heart. After prayer the subject I addressed the people from, is recorded in the gospel by St. John, chapter 3, verse 3, "Jesus answered, and said unto him, Verily, verily, I say unto thee, except a man be born again, he cannot see the kingdom of God."

In addressing the congregation, my heart was greatly enlarged, my zeal inflamed, and my desires running out after the salvation of souls in such a manner that I have often thought, that had I had twenty tongues to have employed that day, I should have had subject matter for them all to improve from. I dare not say but I had some sweet thoughts that God would raise me perhaps to the ministry; but against them I struggled, and would not give them entertainment in my heart under the apprehension that they were the productions of pride. However, it was a full day of comfort to us who were banded together in love, and also of deep humility to myself.

After the meeting was over, one of the auditory solicited me to retire with him and informed me, "That if ever he possessed the assurance of faith in his life, he did when I was speaking under so full a gale as he apprehended me to be." This passage, also, came home with assured confidence to his soul, "I will raise you up a prophet of your own, until him shall you hearken." The passage he understood, as having a reference to me, as the person that would be raised up, etc.

The consequence of this day's meeting was, that several of the congregation requested me to speak at their houses, and the encouragement my friends gave me to the same effect was, that it should be several times a week.

Chapter 2

The author goes to hear Mr. Pickett preach in Culpeper, who is accused by the Church Parson there of preaching false doctrine; Mr. Pickett vindicates his doctrine in an argument with the Parson. At length our author engages the Parson in an argument on the same subject, and measurably confutes him. On a particular occasion, searches the scriptures impartially, and gets convinced that believers are the only proper subjects of baptism, and immersion the only proper mode.

As to my being set forward to the work of the ministry, according to the rules of the society with whom I soon joined, and of my subsequent sufferings, in order to give a satisfactory account thereof, it will be necessary to mention a number of attending circumstances. I did not view myself as under the character of a preacher at the time my friends encouraged me to visit the neighbouring houses; but as I had been an active leader in vanity amongst them, I concluded that I might endeavour to be as instrumental for their good, as I had been in drawing them into sin.

Hearing that the gentleman who had disappointed us in coming to the aforesaid visit, was to preach about forty miles from us, I was very anxious to go to hear him. There is no necessity to secret his name; it was Mr. John Pickett of Fauquier County; he was to preach at Capt. Thomas McClanagan's. At that time the Church of England Parsons were exalted in domination over all dissenters in the colony, as it was then called, of Virginia. The dissenters had to pay their proportion for the building of churches, and sixteen thousand weight of tobacco annually for the support of those clergymen, exclusive of building their own houses for worship, supporting their own ministers, and being precluded the benefit of marrying the members of their own society, except they procured and paid to the Church Parson of their parish a full marriage fee for each couple. And this galling yoke continued on the necks of the dissenters until some time after our glorious revolution took place.

The Church Parson in Culpeper County had made it a practice, where any of those Baptist Preachers would have an appointment for preaching to go in person to those meetings, taking some aids with him, who were as much prejudiced against that sect as he was. Being a man of rapid flow of misrepresentation and persecution, upon religious subjects, would by his dogmatical manner, appear frequently to an audience he would address, to gain his point and acquire the mastery over his opponents.

This personage attended at Capt. McClanagan's in order to detect the falsity of Mr. Pickett's doctrines before his parishioners. Being acquainted with Mr. Pickett's disposition and turn of mind, I felt very uneasy that day, when I saw the position the Parson took. The place Mr. Pickett was to preach in, was pretty capacious for the congregation; the Parson had a chair brought for himself, which he placed three or four yards in front of Mr. Pickett, on which he seated himself, taking out his pen, ink and paper, to take down notes of what he conceived to be false doctrine. By the countenance of Parson Meldrum's parishioners, they appeared to be highly elated, under an assured expectation of his baffling the New Light, as they called him. I discovered it was some embarrassment to Mr. Pickett, and impeded his delivery, but I possessed a confidence that he preached the truth, and nothing but the truth, which could be supported and defended against its enemies.

As soon as Mr. Pickett had finished his discourse, the Parson called him a schismatick, a broacher of false doctrines, and that he held up damnable errors that day. Mr. Pickett answered him with a great deal of candour, and supported the doctrines he had advanced, to the satisfaction of all those who were impartial judges of doctrine. He was a man slow in argument, and when contradicted it would in a measure confuse him, which I soon observed, by some points he advanced, in which, in my judgment, he was perfectly right. The Parson at the same time, I observed, was taking notes of what the other said, which made me careful to retain it on my memory, standing close by Mr. Pickett when he spoke. The notes the Parson took, were absolutely the reverse of what Mr. Pickett delivered, and the Parson asserting them with dogmatical precision, and his parishioners exulting in the same, I could not forbear immediately interfering.

I addressed the Parson to this effect, "Sir, I presume you will grant the privilege of others hearing and determining as well as yourself: I have got eyes to see, ears to hear, and a judgment to determine with others. With respect to these remarks you have made, upon what you say Mr. Pickett asserted, they are of no avail; he did not say those things with which you charge him, and in justification of what I assert, I could freely appeal to others." He wheeled about on his chair towards me, and let out a broadside of his eloquence, with an expectation, no doubt, that he would confound me with the first fire. I gently laid hold of a chair, and placed myself upon it close by him, determined to argue the point with him from end to end. I am sorry I cannot enter into a full detail of the first argument, as it was very lengthy, and my present low state gives me some apprehension that I may not finish my history; however I shall touch upon it.

Understanding he had been raised a Presbyterian, before he commenced Episcopalian, I formed the plan of entering into a discourse with him. First, upon the doctrines of religion, and secondly, upon the practice of it. This was with a view to endeavour to gain his consent that what he called damnable errors were consistent with gospel principles and practices; which consent I obtained in the sequel. Our first parents original rectitude, their fall and apostasy, their inability to extricate themselves out of that state, the plan of salvation through faith in, the Redeemer's merit, justification before God, through the Spirit in His gracious operations, and the consequence attending the same, viz. life and eternal glory. These were the topics that employed us first. I cannot recollect that he asserted there were any of them corrupt, but at times would endeavour to say, they would admit of a different construction, which construction, when given, I would immediately oppose and support my opposition, both from scripture and the articles of the Church of England. He would appear considerably chagrined at my doing so, and carried an appearance sometimes, as if he would have made me feel his resentment, at other times, in the argument, he appeared tolerably well pleased.

However, I discovered that pursuing the argument was and would be at the risk of incurring the displeasure of both gentlemen and ladies of his society, and perhaps the greater bulk of them. They would look at me with the utmost contempt and disdain, supposing it no doubt, presumption in such a youth as I, to enter into an argument with the teacher of the County. In the course of our argument, they would repeatedly help him to scripture, in order to support his arguments, which made me observe to them that they did not treat me with common justice, that I had none that helped me, whilst they were supplying their Pastor with every help they could afford.

When we got upon the second point, relative to practice, I dressed Mr. Pickett's expressions in other language, but retained the substance of them, and the Parson fell into the gin, by confessing they were truths. Mr. Pickett immediately replied, how could he now confess that to be truth, which he had just before called error, and damnable error, so ended the dispute.

I immediately got up and addressed one of the gentlemen who had been so officious in helping his teacher; he was a magistrate at that time, and one of those who afterwards committed me to prison. I addressed him in this manner, "Sir, as the dispute between the Parson and myself is ended, if you are disposed to argue the subject over again, I am willing to enter upon it with you." He stretched out his arm straight before him, at that instant, and declared I should not come nigher than that length. I concluded what the consequence would be, therefore made a peaceable retreat.

Mr. Pickett's next meeting was to be contiguous to Col. Easom's, in an old field under some comfortable shades. It being on the Lord's Day, the Parson had to attend his parish church, so that we met with no opposition from that quarter, but we it from another; as the congergation was very large, amongst them there were abundance of Negroes the patrollers were let loose upon them, being urged thereto by the enemies and opposers of religion. Never having seen such a circumstance before, I was equally struck with astonishment and surprise, to see the poor Negroes flying in every direction, the patrollers seizing and whipping them, whilst others were carrying them off prisoners, in order, perhaps, to subject them to a more severe punishment. Meeting being concluded, Mr. Pickett, with myself and a number of others from our parts, that had come over to this day's meeting, took our leave of each other that evening, and returned to our respective settlements.

I endeavoured still to improve in the neighborhood where I lived, from the motives and principles heretofore mentioned; but would not admit the idea of the name Preacher, to associate itself with my performance; the word Preacher being too great and sounding a title for me to assume.

A circumstance among our little banded society, on Smith's Creek, produced a degree of trouble and anxiety, for a short time, but happily terminated to our general satisfaction. The circumstance related to myself. The work of God, through the colony of Virginia at that time, was carried on under the ministry of the Baptists. Those Baptists were distinguished by the appellation of *Regulars* and *Separates*. Both parties were Calvinistic in their sentiments, and our little religious body were disposed to join with them, by submitting to the rules of their society, and were fully persuaded that baptism was rightly administered according to the primitive mode and institution, the example of Jesus Christ, and the practice of his apostles, by *immersion* and a public profession of faith in Christ.

In this point they were all of one heart and one mind, myself only excepted. I was still tenacious of the old mode of sprinkling, according to the Presbyterian plan. They apprehended that if any gift was ever raised amongst them it would be me, and if I continued under that persuasion it would be productive of a bar among us. This, no doubt, occasioned many prayers to be sent up by them to the throne of grace on my behalf, in order that I might be convinced of my error in this respect.

Discovering the uneasiness that existed among them led me to search the scriptures impartially, and in a short time it pleased God to remove the scales from my eyes, and give me to see that I must be a partaker of the grace of faith in Christ before I could be regularly entitled, as a subject, to an ordinance of His instituting. The application was very powerful, so that nothing could eradicate it from my heart until I had manifested my obedience to Christ by following Him into the water, and submitting to His ordinance of baptism, and thus putting Him on professionally.

All being now united together in one mind and one judgment, and possessing a warm zeal for the glory of God and honour of our Redeemer, we wished to know which of the two bodies, Regulars or Separates, had the warmest preachers and the most fire among them; we determined in favour of the latter, although the ministry of both names were warm and zealous men.

Chapter 3

He sets off to go to an Association in North Carolina, his horse giving out was like to have prevented him, his business was chiefly to get baptized.

Hearing that there was to be an Association in North Carolina, at a place called Sandy Creek, Shubalstarn (Shubal Stearns) being the stated pastor there; at which place the ministers of the Separate order, from South Carolina, North Carolina and Virginia were to meet, likewise a number of Regular ministers from Virginia. They were delegated from their Association to attend that Association, in order to bring about a union between the two bodies which was not effected at that time, but it was some years afterwards.

The solicitations of my dear friends at Smith's Creek, as well as a consciousness of duty, determined me to attend the aforesaid Association, in order to give them a relation of what I hoped God had done for my soul; there not being an ordained minister in Virginia, of the Separate order to administer baptism, that being also one principal object with me in going there; as also to exercise my gift among them, whereby they might judge of the propriety of granting me credentials to exercise in the ministry. One disadvantage, with regard to this journey, I laboured under: the ministers that went out from Virginia, went together in a body, and had got considerably the start of me to the Association. However, by crossing the country, and obtaining good directions, I overtook them, in traveling about one hundred and fifty miles, in Amelia County, on the other side James River, where they had an appointment for evening meeting.

There was a circumstance happened in this journey that had a strong appearance of preventing me from prosecuting it. I pushed my horse so fast that he gave out. The evening he gave out I put up at the house of a stranger, who acted as a real friend to me. He was a pious member of the Baptist society. After relating to him the flourishing state and prospects of religion at Smith's Creek, the cause of my present journey, and the circumstances attending it so far, I perceived he was sensibly concerned for me, which he fully manifested by his future conduct. After expressing his sorrow, that it was not in his power to help me to a horse himself, he turned out, with great anxiety and assiduity among his neighbours, and procured one for me, in exchange for mine, which I accepted.

The reader must recollect my remarkable dream about my being taken prisoner, etc. This dream seemed evidently to be fulfilling in this journey—Never having traveled this route or course before, I was singularly impressed with my dream, and more especially when I took a retrospect, that I was conducted over two mountains (Massanutten and Blue Ridge I had to cross in this journey) until I came to the little old field, being so admirably calculated to the view I had in my sleep, long before I bore a publick testimony in preaching the gospel. When I had in fact to pass through the little old field, on my way to the southward, I was forcibly struck with the appearance of every thing there, agreeing so well with what I saw in my vision. I looked for the little house I was to be imprisoned in, and saw it in a direction agreeably to my dream. Curiosity prompted me to leave the main road and ride out to it, and look in at a small window, secured with iron grates, under a full persuasion, that I should be brought to suffer persecution, and that *that* small apartment would be the place of my confinement in future. Under these impressions I left the little limbo.

I have already given an account of overtaking the ministers and friends in Amelia County. It happened when the people were assembling for an evening's meeting, and I was agreeably entertained with a sermon delivered by the Rev. Nathaniel Saunders, after riding fifty-five miles that day and ferrying James River in a boat.[14]

---

[14] According to Robert B. Semple, Nathaniel Saunders, spelled "Sanders" in the 1819 edition, was not an especially gifted preacher but he was "sound in the

It now became my duty to give the ministers going to the Association, certain information respecting myself; such as, how far I had followed them in order to overtake them, the motives I had for so doing, etc. They heard me with great complaisancy, and gave me a very Christian reception. Our host was a Baptist. The elder ministers requested me to tarry there that night, where I would be well entertained, and enjoy for my company some worthy young ministers whom I had heard preach the August before, at an Association; and upon my making them acquainted with some of the circumstances thereof, they remembered them, and recollected me.

After we had retired to our bedroom, it was proposed among us that, if none of us were sleepy, we would improve part of the evening for edification, to which we all assented. Our subject was a religious experience. One of the preachers addressed me and the rest of the company to this effect; "Whereas our young friend here, has come a great distance upon laudable principles, and has already given us some account of a gracious work of God going on in his neighbourhood, he would be exceedingly well pleased, provided," he said, "I felt a freedom, if I would communicate to them what the Lord had done for my soul:" bringing in, at the same time, I think that passage of the Psalmist viz. "Come all ye that fear the Lord, and I will tell you, etc." I felt very humble at the time I was giving them (as Peter saith) the reason of the hope within me. They were very much affected with my relation, so much so that one of the ministers embraced me in his arms.

A disagreeable piece of business took place next morning, just as we were going to family worship. Three very dissipated men, who had been at certain race paths in the vicinity early that morning, trying the speed of their horses, came riding up to the porch of the house where we were. Our landlord had no connection with the race paths. One of these men, the most daring in wickedness, most insultingly abused one of the ministers, accompanied with horrid oaths. Another minister reproving him for swearing after he was dismounted and in the porch among us; the ruffian instantly flew at him, seized him by the throat, and choked

---

faith," and willing to face persecution. See Semple, *History of the Baptists in Virginia*, p. 234.

him till he was black in the face; the minister making no resistance, the landlord and I, interfered in his behalf and with difficulty, disengaged the ruffian's hands from his throat. After this, we had no small trouble and difficulty to get rid of this outrageous banditti; but at length we succeeded and they went off apparently both mortified and ashamed.

Chapter 4

In going to the Association he is frequently urged, by other ministers going there, to preach, which he accedes to with some reluctance at first, but finds it proved an advantage to him in the end.

As we purposed collecting all our company together, in order to pursue our journey that afternoon, there being a number from those parts, preachers and laity intending to accompany us to the Association; we had concluded the evening before to have preaching towards the middle of the day at a meeting house, a few miles ahead. This was not only to accommodate the people in those parts, but, likewise, to give our company an opportunity of collecting together. When riding to the meeting house, the ministers urged upon me the duty and propriety of saying a little to the people. I remonstrated against it, knowing that some of the ministers that would be there, were esteemed among the first rate preachers; observing at the same time that I considered my talents as being very small, and never could bear the appellation of preaching to be given to any of my public exercises, but rather that of exhorting. I observed, moreover, that it would be treating the congregation ungenerously to prevent them from hearing a preacher of superior talents, by introducing me: they smiled, and concluded we would leave the event to the Lord.

The person, whose lot it was to preach first that day, was an old veteran in the service of his Master, had been highly honoured of God, in promoting the interest of His kingdom. He feared God, but he feared not the face of man, and could stand up in the cause of his Master, support and defend His truths in the face of any audience. I have heard young preachers say, they would rather any man should be present than that person when they preached, in consequence of the criticizing eye he kept continually fixed upon them. If I spoke that day that was the person I had to speak after; and from the consideration of the great thing it was to be a mouth for God, to speak to the people with the ideas of my weak talents, subjected me at times to despondency. But this much dreaded preacher, proved of greater service to me, as will more fully appear hereafter, than any minister I enjoyed an acquaintance with.

The time for preaching came, and our ancient preacher took his place. His mental abilities were then perhaps, in their meridian, and he delivered a discourse to the general satisfaction of all the pious there present. Of him it might be said, that he brought out of his treasures, things new and old; and that day fed the lambs and sheep of Jesus.

As soon as his discourse was ended, the general application was for me to take the place and address the people. The ministers and elders had fixed it so among them that a negative from me was not admissible. I solicited a few minutes intermission in order to retire and give my mind up to the Lord, being tinctured with a little touch of Quakerism, supposing that if I felt a good frame, (as I then called it) I could with greater freedom go forward. After we had sung and I had made prayer, I addressed the people from 2 Cor. 6:2, "Behold, now is the accepted time; behold, now is the day of salvation." The deportment of the person who preached before me, embarrassed me a little at the beginning, in consequence of his attitude at that time. He placed himself close by the pulpit, his left arm resting on his side, probably for his greater ease, whilst his eye was unabatedly fixed on me. However, in a short time my heart got enlarged, and he sunk before me like a shrub, among lofty cedars. Warm and under the impressions of my first love, the dear followers of Jesus appeared to have their hearts filled with the same sweet sensations that my own was enlarged with.

When meeting was over, and I was standing under some trees with other ministers, they would come and take me by the hand expressing their obligation to God for what they had heard; imploring the Lord in my presence, to support me in the work I was engaged in, with every other necessary encouragement, suitable to my youth and present pursuits.

One of the young ministers took the freedom to expostulate with
the minister who preceded me, to know the reason why he
countenanced[15] me in the manner he did, seeing it might have
subjected me to certain embarrassments. To which he replied, it was
customary for him so to do; that he wanted to try what *mettle* I was made
of, and with a smile told them all, he believed I had very good *bottom*, for
which he was the more attached to me.

As we had day and even night meetings appointed almost the whole
way to the Association, we had to attend them, by which means our
journey was measurably protracted; but care was taken that it should not
prevent our arriving at the Association in time.

I enjoyed great satisfaction with all the ministers, in whose
company I had the happiness to be; but there were two in particular,
who engrossed the greatest part of my conversation. One of them was a
Regular minister appointed by Broad Run Association, to attend the
Association in Carolina, with a view of bringing about a union as before
mentioned. The other was the Rev. Jeremiah Walker, minister of the
Baptist Church in Amelia County.[16] The first was he who I said, proved
so singularly useful to me. The methods they frequently took with me
were as follows. Being inquisitive after further improvement in
knowledge, I would often propose questions to them on points of
divinity, with a view of gaining knowledge. They would answer me in a
remote sense, and tincture it a little with error, with an appearance of
tenaciousness to support it. I, on the other hand, was very tenacious in
defending the doctrines of the gospel, against any thing that appeared to
me to have the remotest tendency to error; having laid it down as a
maxim, to take a truth upon trust from no man. In the conclusion of our
reasoning together, they would with candour and satisfaction, give up to

---

[15] Editorial note in the 1819 edition: Meaning probably, why did he push me
forward to preach so much against my will, or, when the youth was preaching,
why did he look him so steadfastly in the face.

[16] Few mid-eighteenth century Virginia Baptists were more zealous than
Jeremiah Walker. His bold preaching led to the establishment of over 20
churches, as well as time in several Virginia jails. He eventually became a
General Baptist and, sadly, committed some moral indiscretion that tainted his
ministry. See Semple, *History of the Baptists in Virginia*, pp. 28, 171.

the propriety of my arguments, informing me of the motives they had in pursuing these measures with me. Being both considered as able divines, the meetings in the evenings were generally reserved for them, by which means large congregations were collected together. I made it a point chiefly through our journey, to give them my company almost every night, also to attend upon their preaching; but in the last case I was much disappointed in my views, which were to be a hearer, and profit by their superior abilities. Instead of going forward themselves, according to their appointments they often laid it upon me, and would not admit of any apology I would make.

However, they cured me in a great measure of that turn which I called leading towards Quakerism; for it was usual with me, when solicited to address the publick, to say, "I do not feel my mind impressed with the weight thereof; it is not laid upon me at this time, which if it was I should not hesitate." I have no better way of informing you of the method they took to cure me of that weakness, and push me forward to my publick exercises, on all occasions, than by relating the following anecdote. When near the borders of North Carolina, my ancient brother and I were sitting out in the porch of the house, where one of them was to preach that evening. A large congregation were collected to hear, when the minister addressed me thus; "Is it not time for worship to begin?" I replied, I conceived it was, and I wished the preacher that was to go forward, would take his place. He then said, "You are the preacher sir. I told him it was taking me at a very singular disadvantage, as I was not prepared for preaching. He in an affectionate manner told me that I must act like young Timothy, and reprove, rebuke and exhort, with all long suffering and doctrine. I replied that I came out with an expectation of being a mere hearer. His answer was, "I came to hear too." I observed the meeting was appointed for him or Mr. Walker. He said it was so, but I must not expect to get off so, for they had both concluded that I should go forward, and therefore, to prepare my mind, and lay out my accounts for it. Upon that he made some animadversions on a passage of Paul to Timothy, when Paul was exhorting him to be instant in season and out of season, which duly considered, would shew us the impropriety of trusting to our present frames, but we should rather embrace the opportunities providence puts in our way. Under some little anxiety I replied, "Ah, brother Jared, it is not laid upon me, or I would embrace the occasion." Upon that he turned about with a smile, and with the palm of his hand gave me a tap between the shoulders and said, "Now I have laid it upon you, go forward for you need not expect to get clear."

Being pressed into the service of the evening, and not a volunteer, in some dependence upon God, I went forward. My text that evening was, I think, John 5:25, "Verily, verily, I say unto you, the hour is coming, and now is, when the dead shall hear the voice of the Son of God, and they that hear shall live."

Chapter 5

Throng of business at the Association prevents him from getting baptized there, but a way is opened for him to have it done, by going to Mr. Harris's, which he does, gets baptized, preaches his trial sermon, and receives credentials.

In this manner we passed our time and opportunities together, until we arrived at the place for the Association. The preachers to whom I had communicated my intended business at the Association, fully confiding in my integrity and faithfulness to perform my part, and being satisfied with my graces and gifts, never used any other appellation to me than that of brother. A very throng Association we had of ministers and delegates, who came from Virginia and both the Carolinas, and there being a very warm spread of religion at that time, we had previously assigned but a few days for discussing and dispatching the Association business, in consequence of which the ministers had appointed meetings to be attended to on their return homewards. The business however, of the Association, we found to be of more importance than we at first apprehended, which obliged us to attend on the same day and night, without intermission, excepting allowing ourselves scanty repose.

The ministers from the different states were exceedingly satisfied with me and my gifts; got me to attend the stage in preaching to the publick; but the press of business prevented my being baptized, etc. at that time and place, for which they expressed their sorrow. However, the plan for fully accomplishing my objects was formed and communicated to me. Col. Samuel Harris[17] was to be ordained at this

---

[17] Samuel Harris ranks among Virginia's most respected Baptist ministers. Harris had served in a variety of offices ranging from church warden to county burgess. He was converted in 1758, baptized by Daniel Marshall, and began a

Association, by which means the ordinances of the gospel would be administered by him in Virginia, until he received co-aids in the work, and by my riding to his residence where a number of ministers were to attend him, for certain purposes, I could have my own ends accomplished.

He was a great favourite of the ministers in Virginia, and they had planned it among them, that I should be the first person he would baptize. I saw him ordained, and a moving time it was. He was considered as a great man in the things of time and sense; but he shone more conspicuously in the horizon of the church, during the time of our sweet intercourse together, so that he was like another Paul among the churches. No man like minded with him, who like a blazing comet, would rush through the colony or state displaying the banner of his adorable master, spreading his light and diffusing his heat to the consolation of thousands.

When the Association concluded, we took our course for Pittsylvania County in Virginia, until we arrived at Mr. Harris's residence. When Col. Harris was a member of the Virginia legislature he was disposed to figure in high life. His old house, though a very good one, did not answer his wishes; he therefore constructed one on a more elegant plan; but, by the time he had finished the out works of it, it pleased God to convert his soul, and he appropriated or converted his new building into a meeting house. The Baptist church met there for government and discipline; and their preaching was statedly there. The Rev. Dutton Lane was their stated preacher or pastor; Mr. Harris never being ordained till the late Association, nor would he then except of the pastoral care of a church, his work under God being of a more extensive nature.[18]

---

distinguished career as a Baptist minister. See James B. Taylor, *Lives of Virginia Baptist Ministers*, Second edition, (Richmond: Yale and Wyatt, 1838), pp. 28-37. See also Semple, *History of the Baptists in Virginia*, pp. 17-22.

[18] Originally from near Baltimore, Dutton Lane preached with great zeal. He was baptized by Shubal Stearns in 1758 and may have started the first Separate Baptist church in Virginia in 1760. See Semple, *History of the Baptists in Virginia*, p. 17.

Three days and greater part of the nights were employed in preaching to the people at Mr. Harris's; many of the hearers having come great distances. I occupied my part among the preachers. The third day, the whole body of the church went into their meeting house, and according to their rules, sat as a Church to hear experiences and receive subjects for baptism. I endeavoured to make them acquainted with what I hoped the Lord had done for my soul, and with my desires of submitting to an ordinance, in the way that God Himself had instituted it, and which Jesus Christ His Son had sanctioned, when He came from Galilee to Jordan and was baptized of John therein, setting an example for His followers.

After some short interrogations, only for the satisfaction and edification of the church, they gave me the right hand of fellowship, and declared me to be a proper subject for baptism. Next day in the afternoon, was appointed for the administration thereof; it being Sunday, we were to meet very early in the morning for preaching, eleven ministers being there with other inferior gifts. Considering the distance I lived from there, it was proposed among them, and acceded to, that I should preach my trial sermon, and obtain credentials. However, I was tried indeed, thinking they laid too great a burden upon me that day. They got four of their ablest ministers to preach before my lot took place; and being but a young soldier concluded I had not as many rounds as they to fire, that having generally preached in a constant manner through my journey, my ammunition must be nearly expended.

Worship began about 8 o'clock in the morning, the sermon was from these words, Ephesians 2:4, "By grace are ye saved," etc. The second sermon was on a subject which displayed the love of Christ, in dying for sinners. The third, was from these words, "What think ye of Christ?" wherein was opened up His mediatorial characters, His relation to His church and people, and His excellencies and perfections in a beautiful manner. After some intermission, the church and people came together for the fourth discourse; the text respected Christ's dying for our offences and rising again for our justification. In opening of which the preacher got confused and entangled; I beheld it in an instant; this passage of scripture dropped into my mind, viz. "If any man be in Christ, he is a new creature, old things are passed away; behold, all things are become new," (2 Corinthians 5:17). The impression it had on me, disposed me to lay hold of his coat tail and give it a pull, indicating that if he would resign I would take his place, which he understood and motioned an assent to it. I was greatly enlarged on the subject, and gave universal satisfaction to the ministers and society.

Divine service being over, we repaired to the water for the administration of baptism. Mr. Jared was to open up the nature, end and design of the ordinance, and Mr. Harris was to administer the same, which accordingly was done; a solemn surrounding audience attending on the occasion. Next morning I had taken my leave of that church, and I obtained my credentials, signed by eleven ministers, in order to go forward as an itinerant preacher without any hesitation until further occasion.

Here, in this journey, my remarkable dream kept opening up by its accomplishment. I saw therein that I was not to accomplish the business of my southern journey, where I first intended to do it, but had to take another route to accomplish it. I saw a large house, which they called a church, round the outside of which I walked three times and then went in at the door. This last part appeared to be fulfilled in my being three days about Mr. Harris's meeting house, and being received into the fellowship of the Baptist church the third day in the afternoon, and accomplishing all the purposes of my journey before I left there.

Chapter 6

On his return home, he goes through Amelia and Spotsylvania Counties and preaches; also by Culpeper Court House, and takes another view of the little jail there, and turns to Smith's Creek, and preaches a while among them: but business soon takes him into Fauquier and returning thence through Culpeper, is taken up and put in jail.

Being obliged to return through Amelia County (my horse having got a sore back and there I was to receive him again) several meetings were given me to attend on my way thither, to supply vacancies of my brethren, who had appointed them but could not attend them. An affectionate leave of my brethren I took, with their prayers to God for my success and prosperity. The day I came to Amelia there was preaching appointed at the Baptist meeting house; there Elder Jeremiah Walker was to be the preacher, the lot however devolved on me to preach to the people. After meeting I took an affectionate leave of the brethren there, and bent my course homewards; I passed through Spotsylvania and preached to the Baptist church there: a warm and zealous people I found them to be. Next morning I proceeded on my way through Culpeper: and when I passed the courthouse, was impressed in the same manner as formerly—rode out to the little jail, under the impression that I should certainly suffer persecution, and that the man on the red horse would deposit me there, although I did not expect it was so near at hand as it proved to be.

When I returned to Smith's Creek, it was a joyful meeting among my friends. What time I had to spare I occupied among them: but a circumstance occurred, which led me off some distance from them; it was a requisition of a body of Christian men and women who had been brought to the knowledge of the truth by Mr. Pickett's ministration, to whom Mr. Harris, when he got ordained, was to pay a visit, baptize them, and constitute them and us into a church. Brother Harris was to bring other helps with him; and he earnestly solicited my particular attendance there at that time. The meeting was to be held on Carter's Run in Fauquier County contiguous to Culpeper.

The news passing through Culpeper that I was to be down, and that it was expected I would preach in Culpeper on my return home, I received information that I should be taken up and sent to jail. On my way to Fauquier I preached at Col. Pugh's, went home with, and lodged at Col. Tipton's that night. He requested that on my return home I would call at his house and give them a sermon. Having had a familiar acquaintance with him, I modestly looked him in the face, and with a smile told him, that I expected to be a prisoner for Christ in Culpeper jail. I opened up to him my dream, and the circumstances so far attending the same; also the dispute between the parson and myself, and threatenings, in consequence of my purpose to give them a sermon on my return. I delivered my opinion to him on this head almost dogmatically, for the reasons above mentioned. All that he requested of me then was, that I would call upon him and preach among them when a way was opened. This gentleman if living or his family (some of whom of a religious character) could attest these facts.

Through kind providence I attended the meeting at Carter's Run, when, after congratulations together, we retired in order to consult what measures we were to pursue. A certain body of us who had made a public profession of our faith in Christ, being authorized by the different churches or bodies to which we belonged, met as aids at this place, formed ourselves into a church, in order to hear and receive such as we deemed, in a judgment of charity, to be qualified subjects for baptism.

There were between twenty and thirty then received and baptized. Other requisite duties being attended to we proceeded, after a short intermission to constitute the church. The body of the male members possessing a tolerable acquaintance with church government and discipline, and no less than five gifts then existed among us including myself, before we parted that evening in great love and affection, we had the Lord's Supper administered among us.

The end and design of our meeting being accomplished at Carter's Run, I went on that evening to Capt. Thomas McClanahan's, a worthy gentleman at whose house I had the dispute with the church parson; there I was informed that if I preached next day at Mr. Manifa's, I should be taken by Squire Strother and Squire Slaughter. I sat down and counted the cost, freedom or confinement, liberty or a prison; it admitted of no dispute. Having ventured all upon Christ, I determined to suffer all for Him. Next morning I sat off for Mr. Manifa's, at whose house I was to preach, accompanied with the Capt. and his whole family. When I arrived at the place of preaching, Mr. Manifa addressed me thus, "Sir, you may expect to be taken up today, if you preach, a certain fine (I am told) will be imposed upon you, and so much upon each individual that will attend your preaching, as well as a fine of twenty pounds on me for granting you my house to preach in. This the justices have made me acquainted with, and have advised me for my own advantage, not to suffer the meeting."

Mr. Manifa being a man under awakening impressions, told me not to flinch from my duty, if I thought it a duty, to go on. I requested him to shew me the line of his land, ordered a table to be taken out and placed with its feet on each side of the line; whether it might have answered any purpose or not, I cannot tell. However I told him, that when I stood on the table I would not preach on his land no more than on another's.

Preaching being over, and I concluding with prayer, heard a rustling noise in the woods, and before I opened my eyes to see who it was, I was seized by the collar by two men whilst standing on the table. Stepping down off the table, and beholding a number of others walking up, it produced a momentary confusion in me. The magistrates instantaneously demanded of me, what I was doing there with such a conventicle of people? I replied that I was preaching the gospel of Christ to them. They asked who gave me authority so to do? I answered, He that was the Author of the gospel, had a right to send forth whom He had qualified to dispense it. They retorted upon me with abusive epithets, and then inquired of me if I had any authority from man to preach? I produced my credentials, but these would avail nothing, not being sanctioned and commissioned by the Bishop. They told me that I

must give security not to teach, preach or exhort, for twelve months and
a day, or go to jail. I choose the last alternative. The magistrates then
addressed their neighbours and informed them that they were open to
law, but there the preacher stands on one side, and here we stand on the
other; and as we believe you have been deceived by him, if you will
confess it by coming over from the side where he is, to our side, we will
take that act as your concession, and the law will not be put in force
against you. The people were much incensed against the magistrates,
and told them that they had heard nothing preached but the gospel of
Christ, and that if they had not money to pay their fines, they were
willing to go to jail also. The magistrates were much mortified at seeing
the ill will they had got from their neighbours, and their ignorance
being by me, at the same time exposed before the congregation.

I gave security to attend court in a few days, which I accordingly
did. By the complexion of the court I saw there was no liberty for me.
There were eleven magistrates sat as a quorum. They brow-beat me,
mall treated me, and throwed out the most opprobrious appellations
against me—would admit of no defense I could make, but ordered me to
hold my tongue, and let them hear no more of my vile, pernicious,
abhorrible, detestable, abominable, diabolical doctrines, for they were
nauseous to the whole court. I found it of no consequence to defend
myself any further, since imprisonment was inevitable, and they were
determined to make an example of me.

I delivered up my riding horse to a friend to take care of him that
night, and apply to me next day for further instructions. The sheriffs
were ordered to attend me to my little limbo, with a considerable parade
of people, with such vollies of oaths and abuse as if I were a being unfit
to exist on the earth. A very uncomfortable night I passed, in
consequence of the oaths, etc. that continued through the same. Sticks
and stones they were throwing during the whole night upon me.

Chapter 7

He feels his dissolution speedily approaching, whilst giving this relation to the writer, therefore leaves out many circumstances—Relates the doubts he had whilst in jail, with regard to his call to the ministry, but by the application of scripture suited to his case, he becomes fully confirmed in that call.

I have been under the necessity several times of abridging or leaving out several circumstances in this relation, in consequence of my weakening so fast; but now apprehending my dissolution speedily approaching, I cannot enlarge on my sufferings in jail. I shall divide the whole of it into three parts. First, when and how I got established in my call to the ministry; second, my sufferings when in prison, and third, my deliverance therefrom.

When first imprisoned, I entertained a persuasion and belief that I would be singularly upheld with suffering and supporting grace, but I had not been there long, before it pleased God to withdraw from me the amiable light of His countenance; in consequence of which, I got into doubtful disputations about my imprisonment, and whether I was truly sent of Christ to preach the gospel or not. If I thus suffer for His name and cause, why is His presence withdrawn? Grievous and distressing were the days and nights that I then passed, being solicitously anxious to know the mind of the Lord therein, at last unbelief prevailed, and I concluded the Lord had not sent me to preach His gospel, or I would not have been shut up in spiritual darkness as I was.

I concluded then to send for some of my friends, and give the bond required for my liberation. I sent and they accordingly came. They felt sorry for what I was about to transact, but was willing to leave it to my own choice. Discoursing a little with them on former reliefs out of trial,

and my present exercises, it pleased God to let in a glimmering ray of
comfort upon my mind; I grasped at it like a man when drowning,
grasping at a twig, and immediately told the brethren, I could not sign
the bond for my liberation. They went away with grateful hearts to the
Lord for His present interposition. I have called it a glimmering hope,
because I soon fell into doubts again; the exercise of my mind was in
this manner; that if the Lord had not sent me to preach His gospel He
would make it manifest to me, but if He had sent me, and that I was to
suffer in His cause, He would establish me therein.

One day in deep distress, I was lying on my bed, with my pocket
bible in my hand, and praying thus, "Lord if Thou hast not sent me to
preach Thy gospel, convince me thereof, I will come out and take
public shame upon myself, and acknowledge before the world, I had run
before I was sent." Mark what followed. "But if Thou hast sent me to
preach Thy gospel, manifest the same to my soul, let me know the
truth and be free from this distressing temptation." In an instant it
seemed as if the Lord by His Spirit moved upon me, and my mind was
fixed in this manner, that I should just open the bible, and whatever
presented itself to my eye, should be the message of the Lord to me.
The passage that presented itself was, "If you continue in my word, you
shall know the truth, and the truth shall make you free" (John 8:31-32).
So applicable and pertinent was the answer to my prayer, that my chains
in an instant dropped off, my heart bounded with comfort, and if all the
ministers and people of God upon earth, had said I had run before I was
sent, it would have had no influence upon me. The passage opened to
me thus. That it was my duty to continue in preaching His word, and
while so doing, He would make manifest to me the truth of what I
prayed for, and the truth would make me free from such temptation.

I continued in the strength of these comforts three days and
nights, at length that passage was applied powerfully to my soul, with
great comfort, which is in Acts 26:16, "But rise and stand upon thy feet,
for I have appeared unto thee for this purpose, to make thee a minister
and a witness, both of these things which thou hast seen, and of those
things in the which I will appear unto thee." Here did I arrive at a full
and assured confirmation of the Lord's calling me to the ministry of the

word; and I will leave it to every pious soul to form a judgment of what my comforts must have been at that time and in such a place.

Chapter 8

His persecutions and sufferings in prison—receives and writes several letters—he receives many tokens of the divine goodness, so that his prison becomes in that respect, as it were a palace.

Having now given a relation of my call to the ministry, and the comfortable establishment of my mind in said call, I proceed, *Secondly* to give a relation of my sufferings in prison.

The jailer being an avaricious person, and easily perceiving that he had a majority of the people of note on his side, laid down and pursued the following plan, with respect to me. Finding I enjoyed the affections of those people called the Baptists, who were very desirous of coming in to see me, and tarrying all night with me, he would admit none of them to the enjoyment of that favour, without paying four shillings and eight pence. He said they must come in as debtors, and go out as such released: and this sum he called commitment and releasement money. When he happened to have some unruly persons at his tavern whom he wished to get rid of, he would favor me with their company, without any expense, excepting that of suffering personal abuse from them; which some of them were not backward, liberally to bestow. I have had to pay the sum more than once for a single individual, in order to give them an opportunity of laying open to me the state of their souls.

My friends round the courthouse, supplied me amply with wood, it being an extreme cold winter, and a great demand for it. My wood was exhausted very fast, and I as often supplied. The tavern-keeper (who was also jailer) was obliged to furnish me with victuals, and water to drink; but my portion of the latter was scanty enough, in consequence of a scorching fever, which attended me in the night: and, as to the former I had but little recourse to it, as I chiefly subsisted on what my kind friends sent me, or what I purchased with my own money.

When I would be preaching through the little iron grate, the wicked and persecutors would ride up at a gallop among my hearers, until I have seen persons of respectability under their horse's feet: clubs have been shaken over the heads of other individuals, with threatenings if ever they attended there again; whilst the poor Negroes have been stripped and subjected to stripes, and myself threatened with being shut up in total darkness if ever I presumed to preach to the people again.

To such a height of arrogance and wickedness have these miscreants went, that when I have been engaged in preaching the gospel of my dear Redeemer to the people, they have got a table, bench, or something else, stood upon it, and made their water right in my face!

A number of my persecutors resorted at the tavern of a Mr. Steward at the courthouse, there they plotted to blow me up with powder that night, as I was informed. The person employed to provide the materials, lived about twelve miles from there, and on whom the awful judgments of God was soon afterwards manifested, as will be seen hereafter. All the powder they could collect (according to my information) was but half a pound: they had fixed it for explosion, expecting I was sitting perpendicular over it, but in this they were a little mistaken. Fire was put to it, and it went off with a considerable noise, forcing up a small plank, from which I received no damage. I was singing a hymn at the time the explosion went off, and continued singing until I finished it.

The next scheme they pursued was to smoke me with brimstone and Indian pepper. They had to wait certain opportunities to accomplish the same. The lower part of the jail door, was a few inches above its sill; when the wind would be favorable they would get pods of Indian pepper, empty them of their natural contents, and fill them with brimstone, and set them a burning, so that the whole jail would be filled with the killing smoke, and oblige me to go to cracks, and put my mouth to them in order to prevent my suffocation.

At length a certain doctor and the jailer formed a scheme to poison me, which they actually effected, and which I could clearly demonstrate was it expedient, considering my present state, to enter into a full detail of the circumstances. I picked as much out of themselves; and the physicians who afterwards attended me on the occasion, declared it to be so, from the symptoms they saw on me. I was then to be highly favoured by my very enemies, (or rather they pretended so) being opposed to that avaricious gratification, arising from the four and eight pence commitment fees, they enjoyed very little advantages from that quarter; but now I was to be a prisoner at large. I was to go to the doctor's house, (who was in Co. with the jailer) to live there, where every attention was to be paid to me, requisite and proper to my situation. Avarice was at the bottom of this scheme, and I saw through it, and of consequence rejected it with horror. It originated through the affectionate desires of a few of my able friends on Shenandoah River, who in the tavern said, "If there could be any person found, who might be instrumental in restoring me to my health again, and who would get me out among them, they would give two hundred pounds, for bringing about such a favour." Being informed of this generous proposal, as soon as they came to the jail, I gently reproved them for it, and told them I could not come out upon any other terms, than what would comport with the honour of that cause for which I suffered.

Thus, I have given some account of my personal sufferings, to which might be added a hundred circumstances more. Such as being threatened, and expecting every court to be brought out to the whipping post, and suffering there in a public manner, before the gazing multitude. I sat down and counted the cost, believing through Christ's strengthening me, I could suffer all things for His sake. It appeared that their power did not reach so far, or it would have been executed.

Some curious anecdotes transpired in this period, respecting men in a state of intoxication (that were abusive at the tavern, and to get clear of such company, they were locked up with me) of their pretending to be religious when they came in groaning and sighing, when they had no knowledge of what it was about; of the methods I took to sober them, and when effected, the mode I pursued for their mortification and conviction. I must remark that these were not naturally of the abusive kind, that I had the company of, but were such as would thank me for my kindness to them, in the morning when they took their leave.

At this period I received and returned a number of letters from and to the ministers of our persuasion, and from a variety of churches, with whom I was connected. From these churches, I received general information, how singularly these letters were under the kind dispensation of divine providence, blessed to the conversion of numbers of souls, who were anxiously led to enquire into the cause for which I proffered, as well as the grounds of that fortitude which bore me up under these sufferings. My prison then was a place in which I enjoyed much of the divine Presence; a day seldom passed without some signal token and manifestation of the divine goodness towards me, which generally led me to subscribe my letters, to whom I wrote them, in these words, "From my Palace in Culpeper."

Chapter 9

There are two circumstances which the author cannot consent to pass in silence—The first was a letter he received from a certain minister, which was signally blessed to him, and is as follows.

Dear Brother,

I am told that you are honoured with a prison, if it is for Christ, it is an honour indeed, but if for Satan or self, a very great dishonour.

I am informed that you not only preach Jesus Christ as a Saviour, but as a Judge also, and for that reason must love you as a fellow labourer in the gospel. I have nothing at present to add for your consolation, for God has said enough in His word to comfort His people on all occasions, and I hope you are not without a bible, and if you are led by the Spirit of Christ, you then possess the same Spirit of Him who is the Author of it.

O brother, if you can, by bearing the charming, lovely cross of Jesus Christ, win one of the strongest of Satan's strong holds, no matter then how soon you die, and if you thus die for Him, how would the glorious armies of the Martyrs above, shout to see Ireland coming from a prison to reign with them in glory. He then concludes with assurance of his respect for me etc.D. T.[19]

The other circumstance relates to a person I found in jail, when I was put in, and who I believe was a runaway. He was at first a very troublesome person to me, but afterwards became a comfortable one; which when related, it may be seen, bore a near affinity to Theophilus

---

[19] D. T. is probably David Thomas. A well educated, warm hearted preacher, Thomas's encouraging words to Ireland were born from his own experiences. See Taylor, *Lives of Virginia Baptist Ministers*, pp. 41-44.

[Onesimus?] Philemon's servant. He was by birth a native of old Ireland, by profession a Roman Catholic, stocked with as great a measure of ignorance, as ever I knew a man in my life. By stature he was of an enormous size, by look and aspect possessed every appearance as if he could with ease, and without the least remorse, according to their principle in former times, put a heretick to death. This was the person designed to be my steady companion, during the whole of my imprisonment.

I never had any desire to make myself acquainted with the grounds of his imprisonment, although I learned he was a runaway, and had experienced severe treatment, as his back testified to me. One thing I desired respecting him, and that was, if I could be any way serviceable to his soul and body, while together, I would lay myself out for it, but one singular disadvantage I laboured under was, that he imbided the same prejudices against me within jail, as the persecuting mob did without. When his heart in future got impressed, he would confess to me that for some days after I was put in prison, he would look at me with envy, and curse me in his heart.

He was very desirous to make his escape out of jail, and it was in his power so to do, by picking up the brick about the hearth, and making a way to the underpinning, and thus opening a passage for his exit, had not I prevented him; who, in return, threatened to take my life if he died for it. I well knew the reproach of his escape would be charged to me, or why did he not effect it before I was put in jail; therefore I wished to prevent it. He made the attempt and to work he went, when the people in the vicinity of the jail, he expected were all asleep. I immediately told him I would call the people, and alarm them of his purpose; then it was he threatened my life. I saw and felt myself in a critical situation, begged of him to put off his purposes a little longer, and I would endeavour to be his friend in every respect.

Next morning, feeling the effects of the cold, rented myself a very good bed and furniture, at five dollars per month; when he lay upon a raw cow hide upon the floor, sustaining the cold air which had access to him from every direction, without a cover over him. In order to gain his good will and affection, I was studying how to give him the enjoyment of a birth in bed with myself; but he was very dirty, and I rather feared had such companions as are said to be produced by dirtiness, and my delicate taste could not take up with such a partner. Perceiving he had two pretty good shirts, I told him I pitied him on account of his cold birth, and was willing to make that as comfortable as I could, provided he would not take offence at my liberty. I told him of my delicate taste, and that we must have his linens etc. washed, which we soon got done. I took him then as a partner into bed with me, and soon found that the comforts he enjoyed from his new birth, had gained me his affections.

The first discovery I had of his attachment to me, was in his resenting injuries done, or attempted to be done to me. It was not uncommon for persecutors to reach their hands and arms through the grates to lay hold of me, and he stood there ready to resent it; seeing I bore with patience their insults, he could not; for as soon as he could get a chance, he would reach his hand through, and if he caught them by the hair of their heads, he was sure to bring it with him. I used to remonstrate against his conduct, and he would reply, if I would not take care of myself, he would endeavour to take care of me.

I admitted him to my table; and comparing the fare he enjoyed before I was put in jail, with what he then had, he daily fared sumptuously. Evening and morning we would make a little body to address God, by singing, reading the scriptures, and prayer. I took as much pains with him, as ever I did with any mortal in my life, in order to instruct him, and make him sensible of his sinful and guilty state by nature, which in process of time took place. When I would be engaged on my knees in prayer to God, he would pray in a tongue with which he was unacquainted, being the paternoster in Latin. I pointed out to him the impropriety of praying in a tongue he did not understand, and consequently in which he could not open his real complaints to God. He asked me how he should pray. I told him that when I was engaged in that duty, he should give up his heart to God in it, and whatever part was applicable to his state and condition more particularly, he should give his assent thereto. But so far did he deviate from that rule, that he would express himself vocally, every word that he understood. I had to correct him in this precedure also; and then he pursued a more rational plan of conduct, without any further instruction.

I have already observed, that this man was extremely ignorant. The fact was, he was not acquainted with a single letter of the alphabet! I undertook to learn him to read, and drew out an alphabet for him; which, when he had learned, I sent to the store and purchased a testament for him; and he was so ready at receiving instruction, that in a less time than could have been expected, he acquired a capacity to read both the Old and New Testaments, and could quote passages from either, in support of a point of doctrine, in a very pertinent manner.

He became the most assiduous, the most humble and complaisant creature towards me, that could be imagined, in consequence of my kindness towards him, and the spiritual advantages I had been of under God to his soul. He also became deeply impressed with a sense of his state and condition as a sinner. I have laid in secret silence, as if asleep, and heard him get up privately from my side; and for a considerable number of times in one night, heard him imploring, on his bare knees, for mercy from God to his soul, through a Redeemer. Though I left the prison and him behind me, I have every reason to hope and believe, that there was a real change wrought in his heart, by the Spirit and grace of God.

I left directions with him, that if ever he was released from jail, (which he shortly after was) and wished to see me, he would find me at Mr. Jackmon's on Smith's Creek, as my home was or would be there; or, at least, he might get intelligence there where I was. I received information of such a person being upon the inquiry after me, but I never saw him more; yet I hope to meet him, where pain and sorrow will be no more.

Chapter 10

Two circumstances more, before his trial and release from prison. He gives bond and security to appear at the May court, and then takes a journey to Williamsburg, returns and attends his trial, which ends in the mortification and disappointment of his enemies.

Before I give an account of what immediately preceded and attended on my final trial, (if it may be called by that name) and my releasement from prison, I shall give a short relation of two other circumstances, that happened during my imprisonment.

The first respects the person who went twelve miles one evening, as aforesaid, for the powder to blow me up, and on whom the judgments of God were manifested soon after. He with other two young men, went to the back woods to spend some time in hunting. As they three lay by the fire, with their feet towards it, there came up a mad wolf, and although my persecutor lay in the middle, singled him out from the other two, bit him in the nose, of which bite he died in the most wretched situation of the hydrophobia, or canine madness.

The second circumstance was, my bringing over a most violent persecutor to be my friend, to wit, the tavern keeper, at whose house the plot was laid for blowing me up, and who was himself one of those active persons in riding over the people and treading them under his horse's feet. He, with a number of his accomplices, were at the jail window going on with their abusive language, when he applied to one of his companions for ten shillings, as he wanted some more necessaries against court for the tavern. He could not obtain that small sum from any of them, although they were generally applied to. I stepped to the window with the money in my hand, and addressed him thus: "Mr.

Steward, I have heard you applying to your friends for ten shillings, and although unapplied to, I rest in your honesty, here it is, if you will accept of it, and at any time hereafter when it suits you to return it, you may do so." He accepted of it immediately, and struck with apparent astonishment and confusion, he made a kind of a bow and retired.

I perfectly gained him over to be my friend from that instant, neither would he suffer any person to throw out a word of insult against me from that time, without his resenting it. He and his companion would repeatedly apply to the jailer for the key, in order to come in and visit me, at which times we often spent many hours together in friendly conversation.

As to my liberation from prison, there need be but little said about it being some time early in April, and the time of my next trial being at grand jury court in May next, there was a great deal by me to be done between these periods, and but little time to do it in.

The determination of the bench in Culpeper, was to prevent any from preaching in the county, as well as to continue me in prison, in case I did not conform to their terms, which I could not in conscience do. Having continued in jail as long as in my own and the judgment of a number of my religious friends, could be of any further usefulness, before the intended trial I sent for Elder Elijah Craig, and we gave our joint bond, for me to attend my trial at the next term, and so I came out.[20]

Next day I went up to Frederick County, drew up a petition, addressed to Lord Botetourt, the then Governor of Virginia, praying him to grant me the privilege of having a meeting house built in Culpeper County, in order to preach at and in, without molestation, on condition of my conforming to the rules prescribed for Protestant dissenters. To this I obtained the signature of a number of respectable inhabitants, both of Frederick and Culpeper Counties.

---

[20] Elijah Craig and his brother Lewis may have been the most outspoken, and most despised, Baptists in eighteenth century Virginia. They ultimately led a Baptist exodus into Kentucky in the 1780s. See Lewis Peyton Little, *Imprisoned Preachers and Religious Liberty in Virginia* (Lynchburg: J. P. Bell Co., Inc., 1938). Passim.

I repaired to the capitol at Williamsburg; the Governor understood was a religious man, and his universal conduct was stamped with the approbation of all, both within and about his capitol. Whether he possessed vital religion or not, I will not presume to determine; but he received my petition with all the graces of a gentleman, and gave me directions what measure to pursue, antecedent to granting the privileges I requested. I found the clergy in the city to be of quite a different character from the Governor; they appeared obstinately determined not to give me the examination I had to undergo, every one shifted it upon another, till at last I obtained it from a county Parson, living eight miles from the capitol, who gave me a certificate of the same. I then returned to the capitol, and presented it to the Governor and Council, who granted me a license for those things petitioned for.

I returned homeward, and with a number of friends attended on the day of trial at the court house. They had found a sham jury against me, determined still to continue me in prison. I was indicted for alleged crimes, which if proven, would have subjected me to criminal punishment. The King's attorney opened up the indictment, and then presumed to ask me, "Guilty or not guilty?" I answered, "Not guilty;" and declared that if five hundred witnesses were not sufficient, I could produce a thousand, to destroy the validity of what I was charged with. Finding them deaf to every thing I could offer in my own defense, I then produced my license, signed by the first authority, to have a meeting house built in that county, for myself to preach there without molestation. Never was a people so chagrined as the bench of magistrates were; however, still they were determined to send me back to jail, and I had to give a friend the charge of my riding horse and furniture. One of my friends at that instant tapping me on the shoulder, asked me if I had any objections to employing an attorney? I answered no, provided he would make good what he undertook. I immediately turned round to lawyer Bullett, (since Judge Bullett) asked him if he would undertake my cause and insure success? He answered in the affirmation. Five pounds (equal to $16.66) being his fee, I agreed to give it.

After a good deal of altercation between my attorney and the court, he told them plainly, that they had prosecuted me upon laws that had no existence these seventy years, that they subjected themselves to a prosecution on account of their conduct towards me, as those conventicle acts were repealed at the accession of William the Third to the throne of England, and had never an existence since.

The county Parson was very officious in giving his assistance to the bench, in the dilemma they were then in. I applied to Mr. Bullett to move the court to give the Parson and I leave to argue the point in hand before them, and if I did not confute him, I would go to prison as a volunteer! He, with a smile replied, "The word of God does not pass current in this house?" I answered, "It appeared so, or they would not imprison those who preached it."

By this time the confusion of the bench was conspicuous to all that were in the house; the judge of the quorum picked up his hat and went out of doors, another followed his example, until the whole of the magistrates evacuated the bench; and there did I stand like the woman accused of adultery, before Christ, who told them, that "They who were without sin, should cast the first stone; when they all went out, being convicted, one by one."

The clerk of the court, in a sham, asked me if I would attend there again, when called for, knowing it was a thing that would never take place. Although I urged at the time, that the court should pursue their object, yet I consented to give them a visit again, when solicited by them, which never happened.

Thus ended this great sham trial, to the mortification of the bench and their abettors; whilst on the other hand, the pious followers of the dear Redeemer were overjoyed at their disappointment, and the prospect of having a meeting house for themselves. Till the meeting house was erected, an arbour was set up, under the shelter of which, other traveling ministers attended and preached to the people in my absence; and this was the first means of the gospel being spread in that county, the happy and astonishing spread thereof, is now conspicuous to all in the county who are religiously disposed.

Now I enjoyed my liberty to exercise my talents through the state, (then colony) for the good of souls.

Chapter 11

The parts of the country, wherein he made his tours in preaching—the general character of the inhabitants—the opposition and success of his ministry—the doctrines he preached—his marriage—and his persecution by a brother in the ministry, etc.

From what has been said, you cannot help taking notice of the awful darkness which overspread Virginia at that time; although in speaking of it more particularly I shall divide it into three districts of country, and touch upon the general character of the inhabitants of each, so far as I was then, and shortly afterwards, acquainted with them.

The first, from the Blue Ridge of Mountains down towards the Bay, they were considered as the politest part of the people, prior to any spread of the gospel therein. Religion was a subject that did not concern their minds, unless it was in their opposition against those who felt the earliest impressions of it; they resigned and gave up their spiritual concerns to the guidance and direction of their spiritual guides: like *priest* like *people*, they appeared all to be in the ditch, put their trust in men, and made flesh their arm. Scarcely a persecution took place, in that quarter, but had a priest at the head of it, and received the hearty concurrence of their parishioners.

In early stages of my ministry, I made a visit almost down to the Bay; in that course of preaching, I traveled a considerable distance, and met with exceeding few that had any desire for the conversion of their souls.

From reasons heretofore assigned in my narration, I shall not discuss the circumstances attending my journey any further than mentioning a few particulars which I shall blend together.

Opposition attended me every where; in the time of preaching, one body of the congregation would be calling out to the other to whip the fellow off the ground; half a dozen of fists would be drawn at a time, when I expected to be knocked down every minute; sailors were brought on shore from their vessels, through the influence of the people, in order to take me out into the stream, hoist me up to the yard's arm and so to give me a ducking. At other places public teachers would, after sermon, introduce controversies, principally on the ordinance of baptism, which I would undertake accordingly to the mortification of those who introduced them; by which their congregations were convinced of the propriety of believing baptism by immersion.

Without any more animadversion, there was always a party in favour of the cause I had espoused; often soliciting me to visit them again: and when ever the Lord was pleased to form any opening upon their minds, it was surprising to see how docile and tractable they were to receive instruction. They were a people possessing good parts naturally; all that they wanted for religious advancement, and divine improvement, was the quickening, awakening, convincing and divine teaching of the Holy Spirit, attended with the heart changing and efficacious grace of God upon their souls, which was opening upon them at that period, and many of them soon manifested divine progress, in the ways of Jesus.

The prisons, in divers places, were honoured with the poor despised preachers: however their situations were much more comfortable than mine; because none were precluded from visiting them; none of those punishments inflicted on me attended them; whilst several of them at a time would be in company together, by which means, they proved a mutual comfort and establishment to each other. By comparing their situation with mine already given, the reader may easily draw inferences from the premises.

Being two hundred miles from my residence, I longed to be back among those called my own people; that being the second division, which lays between the Blue Ridge and Allegheny Mountains. The people inhabiting these valleys, were better informed, arising from the following considerations: they were a divided people as to religious persuasions, consisting of Baptists, Presbyterians, Methodists, Quakers, Menonists, Tunkers and Churchmen, with a variety of others. As persecution was not a reigning principle among them, and they lived in a common state of sociability, it gave them an opportunity of being acquainted with each other's principles and practices, by which their ideas became more enlarged, and their judgments more generally informed than those of the first division.

With regard to the third division, who lived beyond the Allegheny Mountains, in our western settlements, it would be hard for one to give a proper description of them, until time and opportunity of action, would enable such to form a correct opinion. But as kind providence had allotted, under the Blue Ridge, through all the courses and windings of this valley, (between the Ridge and Allegheny) and from the other side of the Allegheny down upon the Ohio, to be the sphere of my ministerial labours, and public services put in my power, were it necessary, I could give a full detail respecting them. When I went among them, I found them to be an uncultivated people; the farther I went back the more rude and illiterate they were: I often thought they constituted a compound of the barbarian and the Indian; although I found among them, a number of respectable and well behaved people; but my present remarks I have given in the gross.

When first liberated from prison, my heart glowed with a zeal for the glory of God, the honour of my dear Redeemer, the prosperity of religious societies, and gathering in of souls to the Lord Jesus. In a dependence on *Him*, I immediately set to work. The doctrines I began first to preach, were our awful apostacy by the fall; the necessity of repentance unto life, and of faith in the Lord Jesus Christ. We being by nature, *dead in trespasses and in sins,* our helpless incapacity to extricate ourselves therefrom I stated and urged. When in the exercise of this duty, I would be at it day and night: preaching three times a day very often, as well as once at night, without any regard to the inclemency of weather, or distance of place, so I could reach it. In a dependence on God, I surmounted every difficulty that lay in the way, without ever sparing my human frame, notwithstanding numbers of my friends would tell me, I would destroy the earthen vessel before my services could be completed. This had no influence upon me; the salvation of precious souls possessed the leading faculties of my soul, and strongly influenced my heart.

As the great God has been graciously pleased, more or less, to honour the ministry He had committed to me, wherever I preached, as soon as I discovered that poor sinners were brought to see their helpless condition to quicken their own souls, I would immediately direct them where their help was to be had, and that it was their duty to be as much engaged for the salvation of their souls, as if they thought they could be saved by their own works; but not to rest upon such engagedness, or trust in their best works, but on the Lord Jesus Christ alone, and His precious merits.

I endeavoured to open up to them those extremes of being saved by the merits of our works, and of our being justified by faith without works. I attempted to give works its proper place and shewed that a good work could not be performed without faith, as Paul expresses to the Hebrews, "For without faith it is impossible to please God." To which agrees the article of the Church of England, where it saith, that "All works done before the grace of God and inspiration of the Spirit, are not well pleasing to God, in as much as they have not the nature of faith in them."

I explained to them the nature of justification, and that it consisted in apprehending the merits and righteousness of Jesus Christ for the same, by a divine faith, which faith was of the operation of God in the heart by His divine Spirit, as you may see in Ephesians 2:8, "For by grace are you saved through faith; and that not of yourselves it is the gift of God." I also observed that this righteousness of Christ on account of which we are justified, consisted in the Redeemer's obedience and sufferings, who having answered the requisitions of law and justice, and the soul brought to venture its eternal salvation thereon, it was God's act to pardon sin and receive the believing sinner into His favour, whereby he stood in a state of acceptance before Him. Romans 5:1-2, "Being justified by faith, we have peace with God, through our Lord Jesus Christ. By whom also we have access by faith into His grace, wherein we stand, and rejoice in hope of the glory of God."

Thus I endeavoured to establish the doctrine of Paul's justification by faith without works, and reconcile it to the doctrine of the Apostle James, who sheweth that faith without works is dead, and that there was no way to prove our faith to be a divine one before God, without its producing these genuine fruits of righteousness that flowed from its pregnant womb. I distinguished between imputed righteousness and inherent holiness, and shewed that the former was connected with justification, whilst the latter flowed from sanctification. I shewed that those whom God justified, them He also sanctified; that sanctification consisted in an internal change of the powers and dispositions of the soul, quickened and renewed, by which the subjects thereof, were transformed from sin, and conformed to God and Christ in the ways of holiness. That such were new creatures, that they had the Spirit of Christ, and enjoyed a participation of the divine nature in its gracious qualities and heavenly dispositions; that a principle of grace and holiness was planted in their hearts, so that it was as natural for them to bring forth fruits well pleasing to God, through a Redeemer, as it was natural for the sparks to fly upwards.

Whenever souls were added to my ministry, it was then, and has been my universal practice since, to inculcate Paul's admonition to Titus, "This is a faithful saying, and these things I will that thou affirm constantly, that they which believed in God, might be careful to maintain good works. These things are good and profitable unto men" (Titus 3:8).

I explained what a good work consisted in, as first that God commanded it; secondly, that the law of God required it, and lastly, that the honour and declarative glory of God should be the end of it. I also explained the difference of the believer in an imperfect state here with respect to the remains of the old man in nature, and the new man in grace, and of the opposition and conflict that often existed between them. That sanctification did not consist in a change of degrees, but only in part through the whole soul, that it was to be a progressive work in the soul, by which we were to die to sin and live to God; which constituted our spiritual warfare whilst here, until the curtain of life was dropped, the being of sin destroyed, and the deathless spirit launched to the realms of glory.

I have only given a brief detail of what I intended to have enlarged upon, the reasons for which brevity, I have frequently hinted at. I will therefore pass this subject by, with making this remark respecting my own judgment thereon, which is, that for a person to make a shining blaze of profession, and speak highly of his justification by faith in Christ, and yet live in the omission and general neglect of the practice of good works, and not be found in the exercise of godliness, it does not appear to me any breach of charity, to believe that such a person never had Christ formed in his soul the hope of glory, or he would be found conforming to every gospel precept, and falling in with every known duty.

Pursuing (as I have observed) preaching day and night, in the early part of my ministry, crying out against the sins of the people, and directing them to Christ the way to God, it may not be amiss to give a short description of my bounds.

From my residence on Smith's Creek, I used to pursue my course into what is now called Rockingham County, from thence take a transition across the Massanutten Mountain, and attended statedly at a place called the White House, where I was instrumental in planting what has been since called the Menonist Baptist Church; from that across the Ridge to the meetinghouse built for me in Culpeper, where under my ministry another church was planted; from thence to Fauquier County, where I constituted another church; thence across by Goose Creek and Berry's Gap to Shenandoah River, where I preached up both forks to the river statedly, continuing so until I arrived at my settled residence. From thence down to Woodstock and Stoverstown; thence over the North, or part of the North Mountain to Cedar Creek, where, in a small distance, about sixty gave in their experiences, from my exercises among them, through the courses I went in that settlement. There were not many places upon the waters, among the back mountains that were then inhabited, but what I visited. Along Cacaphon and the Lost River, from that across the branch mountains; I visited and preached to the people on those waters, Patterson's Creek and the waters of Luna's Creek; thence through the Allegheny Mountains, and preached repeatedly to the people on Dunkard Bottoms. Thence across by Redstone, to the waters of Shirtee Creek, and other places which I cannot recollect. About thirty-six years ago, I baptized there, and constituted a church. The person who made his miraculous escape from the Indians, having been tied to be burned, was a member of that church. The last place I preached at there was Gen. Nevill's. I then bent my course homewards until I got among my places of stated meetings again.

A variety of strange circumstances I met with, during my different excursions through those different tours; but I will not fill up my pages with them at present.

After being engaged, as above, for about one year, I possessed a desire to alter my condition of life. It would be almost like an experience, to give the circumstances attending the same; but I shall only say that the girl, on whom I placed my affections, was the daughter of a Mr. Francis Burgess of Fauquier County. She felt exceedingly near to me, being awakened under my ministry, and, as Paul saith, my child in the gospel. She also experienced her deliverance from under the guilt and burden of sin, under my public speaking. When joined together in matrimony, a most happy companion she proved to me. As her piety and general character is well known in many of the churches, I shall only add, that in every respect she appeared to be a preacher's wife to me. We lived together in a comfortable state for about eighteen years, she bore me eight children, and then was removed by death to a state of bliss where I hope to meet her.

Passing by a number of very striking and remarkable circumstances, relating to my ministry, and which are well known to my confidential friends now living; I shall only add this much, "That the archers shot at me, and grievously wounded me." To explain myself, my meaning is, my popularity excited jealousies in the hearts of some of my ministering brethren. They pursued methods, if possible, to deprecate my ministry; and they were grievously wounding to my spirit; but, here lay the remarkable circumstance attending those designs, that it pleased God graciously to condescend to give me information in the visions of the night, pointing out the persons and the way they were pursuing, by which I was prepared before hand. To a pious minister, now with God, who lay with me that night, I related my dream in the morning. He addressed me with a great degree of tenderness, and said it was of so singular a nature, it must be from God. He requested me to be upon my guard, to depend entirely on the Lord of Hosts, and I would in time see a favourable issue. It was never eradicated from my mind day nor night, until the period commenced to my opposers first design into execution, which ended in his confusion, as well as in my consolation. Tender and delicate to hurt his feelings, I kept it back six months; but it appeared to me, not to be my duty, to hate my brother in my heart, yet I was sensible it was not my duty to suffer sin to lie upon him; therefore, meeting occasionally with him, at a friend's house, I took him out to one side and told him I had got to be a Joseph, a great dreamer, and had a wish to tell him one of my dreams, or language to that import. I related to him from first to last, and waited for a reply. How long it was before he made it, I cannot recollect, but he made me this answer—"That what I dreamed was true," and that the mode of his treating me was consistent with the principles he had possessed and acted from, and manifested towards me. He said he was very thankful that I bore so long with him as I did, as I had it in my power to distress his feelings, and those of many others towards him. He begged of me forgiveness, which I promised, and to forget it if I could, which I said I would endeavour to do also. When we would meet afterwards, he would ask me if I continued in the same mind I was in when we conversed first on that subject. My answer was always in the affirmative.

Desiring to tread lightly on the ashes of the dead I pass this over. And now, as many of my religious friends are fond of poetical compositions, and know that I possess a measure of talent that way, I will entertain them with one in this place. The origin of which belongs to Mr. Thomas Buck Jr. Being at his house one evening, in our younger days, and both being fond of spiritual songs, he mentioned one he would sing; it was called "The Minister's Hymn." After hearing it sung, I observed, I thought it greatly deficient. That the minister's duty, work and reward was but barely touched on in it; but if he would learn me the tune, I would compose him one that would better comport with that title, which was accordingly done, and the hymn is as follows.

1

Ye heralds whose mission from God is to preach,
Appointed by Jesus the nations to teach
The way of salvation, through faith in His blood,
To bring back poor sinners again unto God.

2

Your office is glorious, your work it is great,
The kingdom of Satan through God you must shake;
His strong holds demolish, his subjects subdue,
And bring them at Jesus's feet for to bow.

3

Ye champions of Jesus prepare for the field,
Take hope for an helmet and faith for your shield;
Leave nothing behind of the armour of God,
With tidings of peace have your feet also shod.

4

Thus armed advancing, charge home on the foe,
Proclaiming King Jesus wherever you go;
With courage inspired let nothing dismay,
His merits unfold and His banners display.

5

Deal plainly with sinners and shew them their state,
If dying in sin how unhappy their fate,
If saved through Jesus how blessed their case,
For glory to steer as a vessel of grace.

6

If any despise and the gospel renounce,
The vengeance of Jesus against them denounce,
Proclaim Him their Judge, who's appointed by God
To doom them to hell for condemning His blood.

7

How happy dear brethren will be your reward,
Through Jesus, to bring back a soul to the Lord,
'Twill add to your comfort and brighten your crown
And make it to blaze with eternal renown.

8

Discharging your duty you'll certainly find
The wicked and Satan against you combin'd;
Regard not their malice nor envy, for lo
Your Master is with you wherever you go.

9

Your warfare when ended and foes brought to yield,
King Jesus will sound a retreat from the field;
To glory He'll waft you to dwell with all those,
Whose spirits are blest with eternal repose.

10

In joys that's unbounded a time you will spend,
Till judgment comes on and creation doth end;
Transported with joy at the trump of the Lord,
Your bodies immortal will spring at the word.

11

When saints are collecting and soaring along,
You'll stand in the front of the glorious throng,
And see those dear converts you turned to God
With robes washed white in their Jesus's blood.

12

How ravish'd your souls when you'll hear them thus say,
Dear Master those ministers taught us to pray;
Their conduct, example and preaching the word,
Awakened our souls and turn'd us to the Lord.

13

Says Jesus, this truth I do very well know,
They travelled [travailed?] in birth for your souls here below;
With tears and intreaties oft' begg'd me in pain,
Their labours spent on you might not be in vain.

14

My heralds, my ministers here's your reward,
Come enter, possess the sweet joys of your Lord;
Those mansions of glory shall be your abode,
To shine there like stars of the first magnitude.

15

Judgment being ended, with Christ you'll ascend,
Your glorious Redeemer He doth attend;
With pleasure transcendent free grace you will sing.
In strains of perfection to Jesus your King.

16

Transported in rapture and lost in amaze,
Adoring you'll love, and in wonder you'll praise;
While glorious afresh are presenting to view,
You'll hail the Redeemer eternally through.

Chapter 12

The poisoning of Mr. Ireland and family, with its consequences.

The foregoing part of the life of Mr. Ireland was written by his amanuensis; the low state of his health, after which, rendering it impracticable to proceed any farther, but (although the history is already lengthy) to stop here would be doing the subject great injustice. It would also be depriving the friends of the blessed Redeemer (especially those of them who were personally acquainted with the subject of the history) of a very interesting part of the doings and sufferings of their departed friend.

He was certainly one among a thousand of the ministers of the Lord Jesus, who experienced the extremes of sorrow and joy, of tribulation and comfort. That scripture, Psalm 136:5-6 surely would apply to him. "They that sow in tears shall reap in joy. He that goeth forth weeping, bearing precious seed, shall doubtless come again rejoicing, bringing his sheaves with him."

He certainly sowed much of the seeds of the gospel in weeping and tears, and gathered many precious sheaves of believers in much joy.

And John 16:33, "In the world you shall have tribulation, but be of good cheer; I have overcome the world."

But to proceed; The following account is given, partly from my own knowledge, partly from the information of Mr. Ireland himself, partly from a number of his intimate friends and acquaintances, but mostly from Mrs. Ireland, and from papers found after his decease of his own writing.

Mr. Ireland, after his first marriage, settled on the south or main river of Shenandoah, about two miles above the forks, and lived a while there with a Mr. William Calfy, an old man, who was one of the first Baptists in those parts; and having his wife at home there, he used frequently to go out to preach the gospel of the dear Redeemer, his heart being steadfastly engaged in the work, without any regard to consequences.

From thence he removed and settled high up on Ceder Creek, beyond the first North Mountain. Here he had two children born to him and had a meeting house built here. From thence he removed into Shenandoah County, and settled on land of Charles Buck, near where Water Lick meeting house now stands, where he lived some time. From thence he moved about 15 miles up the south or main branch of Shenandoah River near Colonel Jeremiah McCoy's. At these two places he had his other six children born, by his first wife, at one of which places he lost (by death) one of his children, a little daughter named Letitia, on whom above all the rest, his greatest affections were placed. Here, at the last of those places, he also lost his beloved wife, who died in April 1790.

The next spring he removed to Frederick County on Opequan Creek, and married his second wife the fall following, viz. Miss Ann Pollard, daughter of Joseph Pollard of said county. She was a young lady of fine accomplishments, and proved a mother to his first children. Her mother Frances Pollard was supposed to be one among the first persons who was baptized at the same time she was, and her father was baptized not long afterwards; I have frequently heard Mr. Ireland speak of this wife in high terms of applause.

In June 1792 a shocking and melancholy affair took place in the family of Mr. Ireland.

A Miss Betsy Southerlin, who was then living in the family of Mr. Ireland, had formed a scheme of poisoning some, or all his family; she and Mr. Ireland's black woman Sucky, on their trial afterwards, said it was done through the persuasion of a neighbour.

When the time was come, Betsy made an excuse to go to a Presbyterian sacramental meeting to be held at Opequan meeting house, within about four miles of Winchester, which meeting she accordingly went to. The Monday following she went to town, called on apothecary Sperry for an ounce of arsenick, saying her mother had sent for it to kill rats. The doctor hesitating on the propriety of delivering her the poison before for the above purpose; he then delivered her the arsenick, with which she came home, appeared very solemn, and retired frequently out of sight, and appeared by the looks of her eyes on her returning, as if she had been crying, which induced Mrs. Ireland to conclude she was certainly under conviction. Mr. Ireland came home from Shenandoah County the Tuesday morning following; the family being then at breakfast, with some young ladies in company with them; he was sick, having one of his vomiting spells, a complaint he was much addicted to, as well as that of a flux at other times. He refused to take breakfast just then, observing that his wagon would be along in a very short time, in which was some particular good white sugar, he had bought in Stoverstown, with which he would have his tea sweetened.

The wagon accordingly arrived, breakfast was made ready, and Mrs. Ireland dished out the tea to him. As it was then pretty late in the morning, Mr. Ireland invited her to take a dish with him; she excused herself and drank none; he called his little daughter Jenny to him, observing that she was his favorite girl, and must drink some tea with him, (she was 6, or 7 years old) she complied and drank share of a cup. After breakfast he was immediately taken with a puking, and that violently; it was supposed to be a return of his old complaint, but he grew worse to an alarming degree. The child was suddenly taken nearly in the same manner, turned very pale, and became very limber, not being able to hold up her head; and her eyes turning like a dying person's. It alarmed the family, and all the spectators, especially the timorous and affectionate stepmother, who was then in a state of pregnancy, not wanting many weeks of her time. Sucky, who had a deep hand in the infernal business, in order to do away all suspicion and account for the girl's illness, artfully observed that she had been eating some green apples the day before, (it being some time in June) which was believed, and considered as being the cause of the child's illness. The father suspected at the same time, the child had worms. This continued with her till next morning, in which time it was frequently thought she must ultimately expire.

Mr. Ireland drank plentifully of warm water with a view to work off his vomiting; he got somewhat relieved against evening, when tea was

made again; the two young ladies still remaining at the house, Mrs.
Ireland served the table. Mr. Ireland was generally uniform in his
conduct of eating fast, he soon had two cups drank, and was immediately
taken violently bad, apologizing for his conduct, sprang up from the
table and went out of doors. The family and company were not so much
alarmed as might have been expected, and continued at table. Captain
Pollard, (a brother of Mrs. Ireland's) conceived the tea caused a heat and
burning in his throat and stomach, as though there was pepper in it, and
addressing his sister with a smile, observed there was pepper in the tea;
she said it could not be so, the same having been used before; she asked
the young ladies, if they had any such thoughts of the tea; one of them
said it did seem so. Mrs. Ireland by this time had made a dish for
herself, and had poured a usual quantity into the saucer, and was suddenly
called by Mr. Ireland to come to him. His youngest child, a little boy of
about three years old, called William, though at that time standing at the
table, had not as yet drank any of the tea, did then drink what was in the
saucer. Mr. Ireland grew extremely bad, appeared almost exhausted, and
affirmed that there must be poison in the tea, feeling such unusual
misery, who was then, by his wife, supported to a bed. By this time the
company, who were a short time before, sitting round the table, were all
seized with a violent vomiting, (except Mrs. Ireland, who had only
barely tasted the tea) scattered off from the table, some hanging to the
different door cheeks, and some in other postures, crying out, "Hold my
head, I shall die, give me drink, I am poisoned, etc!"

When the people began to want water Sucky, the black woman,
knowing that her master in particular in his former vomiting spells, was
in the habit of drinking it warm, wished to supply them with the most
effectual kind, viz. some of that previously prepared in the tea kettle, by
putting a considerable quantity of the arsenick purchased by Betsy in
Winchester, into the water and boiling it therein, and which water had
so far been successful with the tea already drank (which was the way the
poison was managed) but fearing a discovery in the tea kettle, she poured
out a tin cup full of what remained therein, and set it by the fire, then
threw the rest out and washed the kettle. Miss Nancy Ireland, (she was
about twelve years old) running to the kitchen to get warm water for
Captain Pollard, from the tea kettle, but finding it empty, took up the

tin from the fire, but the water appearing too hot, and then she hastily pouring in it some cold water, it proved to be dirty, which plainly appeared when brought to the light, consequently she threw the whole away.

Little William was now extended on the floor vomiting as he lay. It was an afflicting and frightful scene to all who knew not the cause, or rather were not agents. Miss Betsy now took an officious part in tending on the sick people, though Sucky did not. They drank much warm water; this scene continued nearly all night, with but little variation. It was concluded the poison must have been in the sugar, as it was the last thing brought home, and there being a report in circulation that the Negroes had put poison in certain sugars of the West India Islands.

About day break all appeared weak, and their thirst and some other sensations being some what abated, they then had a little rest, and some of them dozed. Mrs. Ireland walking out, was asked by Sucky how the sick people were and had been; being told, she lyingly said her black child had been just in the same condition.

A doctor was now sent for to Winchester, which was about six miles, little William and the rest appeared to be better at day break, but he suddenly expired about sunrise in his step mother's lap; he was then discovered to be full of large black spots on his body, many of them as large as the end of a person's thumb.

Between midnight and day break Mr. Ireland grew very weak, and thought he felt the symptoms of death, spoke to Mrs. Ireland (who was frequently at his bed side) advising how she should conduct herself, that is not to take it unreasonably hard, considering the condition he was then in, etc., enjoining her to remember his love to his churches, and tell them he should die strong in the faith he had so long and laboriously been preaching. He still grew worse, his speech became faltering, his eyes dim and even sightless, only as they were opened by his wife, and his hearing confused and indistinct, but his senses remained unimpaired.

In this condition he lay for some time, when suddenly a severe gripe seized him in his bowels; he started up upon his seat in his bed, called for a pot, was helped out of bed to it, when he discharged much black coloured stool, which was frequently repeated to an incredible quantity, after which he experienced some ease.

The doctor came about ten o'clock, he immediately administered sweet oil to the poisoned people, which gave immediate ease. When understanding Mr. Ireland's case in full, he observed, "A mortification took place in his bowels and had it not been for the aforesaid discharge by stool, he must have been a corpse ere then."

The poisoned people still mended by degrees; many people collected at the house; great anxiety was manifested to know certainly how the poison was taken. Col. Mead interested himself in the business, made inquiry in the neighborhood of Newtown and Stoverstown, and of Joseph Stover himself, to know if any bad effects had been experienced from the use of the sugar of the same cask, out of which Mr. Ireland had what he bought; no such thing was experienced. Returning to Mr. Ireland's he insisted on it that the poison must be in the family.

Chapter 13

The examinations, confessions, apprehensions, trials and acquittals of two of the accused, etc.

Sucky the black woman was examined, and pretty soon confessed her own guilt, but did not involve Betsy. She was taken to Winchester for examination, etc. On the way, upon inquiry being made how she came by the poison, she opened the whole secret, and that Betsy had got the poison in Winchester, and it was now hid under a loose stone behind the kitchen chimney.

Betsy was soon after apprehended, and discovered symptoms of guilt. The poison was soon found by the following means. Little Miss Jenny Ireland had been sent by Betsy to fetch her some salt to put in a pone of bread she was about mixing; as she was coming with the salt, she saw Betsy take something out of a rag in her hand, sprinkle it over the pone, then tie up the rag, and hasten it into her bosom, after which she saw her slip into the closet, raise a loose plank, and throw it under.

When she saw the search, under the aforesaid stone (which proved ineffectual) inquiring the reason, and a tied rag was spoken of, she remembered the foregoing circumstance, and told them to look under a board in said closet; they did, but had to use a lighted candle before they could find it. Mr. William Kerfoot was the most active person in finding the poison, examining the suspected persons, and securing them, etc. for which no doubt, he deserves the thanks of his fellow citizens.

It was sufficiently ascertained, by a number of witnesses some time afterwards, that the aforesaid pone of bread was strongly filled with the poison. Betsy was taken in custody on Saturday, but as Mr. Ireland did

not wish to hurry her to jail, but would rather give her friends an
opportunity of seeing her first, she was not committed until Monday.
She confessed the whole crime on Sunday, before numbers, and again on
Monday before Doctor Baldwin, a magistrate in Winchester, and said
she was instigated to perpetrate the horrid crime, as was Sucky likewise,
by _____ and that it was the struggle and remonstrance of her
conscience that caused her to cry the Monday before.

The next county court, Sucky had her final trial and was acquitted,
and at the next fall term for the district court, Betsy had her trial, and
was also acquitted. Six magistrates out of seven were for finding Sucky
guilty, but as the whole bench were not agreed she could not be found
guilty.

Mr. Ireland did not want to pursue the culprit Betsy with rigour, or
he would have employed an attorney against her. And could have brought
more evidence against her; he, in fact, was measureably compelled by
the state's attorney, against his inclination to bring forward his little
daughter Jenny, whose extreme youth was the reason Mr. Ireland was
opposed to her being brought into court; but the attorney, after some
conversation with the child upon the nature of an oath, and what she
knew as a witness, insisted upon her evidence. It was accordingly taken,
and delivered by her in such a sensible and steadfast manner (being cross
questioned by one of the prisoner's attorneys) as to astonish the court,
the bar, and the bystanders, who were very numerous, at the child's
wisdom.

Mr. Ireland continued Sucky in jail some months at his own
expense, hoping to have an opportunity of putting her off, but none
offering, he brought her home, and confined her for a time in his
kitchen loft. Within that time, she got greatly alarmed by her own
accusing conscience, thought and affirmed that she saw the Devil; sent
for Mr. Ireland to come and see her, which he refused to do, without a
second person being with him (lest it should be said by some he had
extorted confession from her). Mr. Joseph Drake being then at Mr.
Ireland's, accompanied him into her apartment, when she criminated
herself in a very high degree, confessing that she was guilty of all that
was charged against her, that she was a murderer, and had murdered his
dear innocent child (meaning no more than that she was privy to, and

had taken an active part in the poisoning business) and requested Mr.
Ireland to have her tried again, that she might make open confession, be
condemned and executed.

Chapter 14

The residue of his labors, misfortunes, sickness and death etc. Concludes with some poems, and a brief account of the deceased's family.

Mr. Ireland's useful labours were not as yet finished; his Lord and Master had still much more for him to do in His vineyard; he pretty soon recovered from the effects of the poison, so as to be able to go about and preach again, not only to churches and congregations that were his more particular charge, but also in the bounds of other churches at some distance therefrom; yet he never fully recovered from the effects of the dreadful poison he had received. Some time prior to his being poisoned, he made a tour to Kentucky, the Canaan of the United States. Here the country appeared so fertile, pleasant and inviting, that as he has since said, he had to make a covenant with his eyes, least he should be tempted to leave his dear people in Frederick and Shenandoah, and remove to Kentucky.

He resisted the alluring temptations, continued faithful to his flocks, though it appeared to make against his temporal interest. After he was poisoned he had the happiness to baptize some hundreds, as may be seen on the record of the Ketocton Association book.

In 1802, in one of his churches only, he baptized ninety-three, fifty-two of which number he baptized in one half hour and a half quarter.

They also complain of the length of time necessarily taken up in baptizing by immersion, let them produce an instance in which so many have been sprinkled in the same length of time by one person.

For brevity's sake we pass over many of the acts of Mr. Ireland's valuable life. In the year 1804, he received a violent fall from his horse;

though for some time previous to that he had commonly rode in a carriage; it happened when he was returning home from one of his meetings; a Negro man, supposed to be in a state of intoxication rode in full force against him; this confined him to his bed for several weeks. Some two or more years after, coming home from Buck's Marsh meeting house in his carriage, it overset near home, by which means in falling therefrom, he was badly bruised and hurt, by reason of which he was soon confined to his bed, and continued so for the most of the time, till his decease. He soon became much swelled in his body, with the dropsy (symptoms of which had appeared for several years past) suffered great misery thereby, lost his appetite, suffered frequently and great pains in his limbs, which was generally thought to be the effects of the poison he had long before received. Besides all this he had excessive scorching fevers frequently.

The dropsy increased and spread; it at length affected his legs and feet in an amazing manner. He constantly refused to be tapped, though he yielded to the use of much Laudanum and Opiom, and other palliative medicines. He had little or no hopes of recovering from the time he was first taken.

In his extreme illness he did not neglect family prayer, etc. as long as he was able to sit up to perform it; and so sweet was the exercise, and so happily was he conformed to the precepts of the gospel, that it must overcome all obstacles and shine after the powers of nature were almost exhausted.

After he had become so weak that he was unable to get out of bed or sit up, he even performed family duty lying, and that frequently. At one time when not quite so low, after having preaching in his own house, he grew so warm in his Saviour's cause, that being helped into his chair, he set up and exhorted the people himself. He bore his affliction with abundance of patience and resignation.

May 5, 1806, he breathed his last, and his immortal spirit we trust and believe, was wafted on the wings of bright angels to the realms of immortal felicity, where he will enjoy the sweet reward of his labours, the embraces of his Redeemer, and the company of saints and angels, singing doxologies to God and the Lamb forever.

The following was published in the Winchester Virginia Gazette, Tuesday, June 17, 1806.

DEATH

Departed this life on the 5th ult. in the fifty-eighth year of his age, Elder James Ireland, Pastor of the Baptist congregations at Buck's Marsh, Happy Creek and Water Lick, in Frederick and Shenandoah Counties, Virginia.

This eminent servant of Christ had laboured nearly forty years in his Lord's vineyard, during a great part of the time, through much infirmity of body, but great strength of mind. He was always distinguished as an able minister of the New Testament, rightly dividing the word of truth, giving to saint and sinner their portion in due season. During his last illness, which confined him to his bed about three months, his mind was tranquil and serene. Fully sensible of his approaching dissolution, and perfectly resigned to the will of God, he endured all things, as seeing Him who is invisible, and having an eye to the recompense of reward, patiently waited for the manifestation of the Son of God, and in full assurance of a glorious resurrection, his mortal body dropped like ripe fruit into the lap of our general mother.

On Sunday the first instant, a suitable and affecting discourse, was delivered at Buck's Marsh meeting house, the place of his interment, to a numerous and weeping audience, by Elder William Mason, from 2 Timothy 4:7-8, "I have fought a good fight, I have finished my course, etc."

FAREWELL GOOD MAN:
A faithful herald thou, of heavenly grace,
Thy life was holy, and thy end was peace.

Mr. Ireland was a man of common stature, straight bodied and limbs, a handsome face, a piercing eye, and pleasant countenance. In his youth he was spare, and used to be called little Jamy Ireland, he was at that time extremely sprightly.[21] But he became by degrees quite corpulent, so that not long after his second marriage, he wanted but

---

[21] Note in 1819 edition: I have been told, by them who knew him well, that during the time of his life of vanity, they have seen him mount a small table, and dance a hornpipe to the greatest perfection.

nineteen pounds of weighing 200[300?]. He was then not only weighty for a horse to carry, but became clumsy in the way of mounting,[22] he therefore when going abroad to preach or otherwise, found it most convenient generally, to ride in his carriage, for several years before his death. The last sermon he ever preached, was at Buck's Marsh meeting house, which was in January 1806, it was on his return home from that meeting, that he received his fall and hurt which caused his death.

As time and opportunity afforded, Mr. Ireland wrote and received a number of letters; his correspondence in this respect being pretty extensive, among the rest, he held some correspondence with _____ But among those he sent, no copies are to be found; but of those wrote to him, some few have been preserved; one, if no more of these is of too great importance to be passed by unnoticed here, as it was written in behalf of, and approved by one of his beloved churches, and which is as follows.

The Baptist Church at Buck's Marsh; to her dearly beloved brother and pastor, Elder James Ireland, who is and has been for some months past confined to his bed, by a languishing sickness and complaints, which appear daily to be wasting his mortal body, and from which, he for a long time, has entertained no hopes of a recovery.

Dear Brother, we most sincerely sympathize with you in your great afflictions, and we trust our prayers to God are, that you may have and sweetly enjoy His blessed presence continually with you; believing that, 'His favour is better than life,' which favour, we have great reason to believe you do graciously enjoy. But dear brother, we must say, that we are afflicted in your afflictions at all times, since you have been confined to your bed; but more so when we meet at the house of God, where your presence often gave us comfort, and your counsel has been as a lamp to light our way. We are ready to say, Oh! That it were with us as in times past, when we were blest, with your labours in the precious gospel of Christ. When we remember those precious and incessant labours of love among us, the great blessings that appear to have attended the same, the many sweet and consolatory seasons we have had in sitting together in heavenly places in Christ Jesus; when

---

[22] Note in the 1819 edition: Rheumatick pains had considerable effect in stiffening his joints.

we with gratitude remember how many precious souls we have seen
coming home to the church, of hearing them tell what great things
God had done for their poor souls, through the instrumentality of your
ministry. And when we further remember, that you have been our
pastor for more than twenty years, and the great love that has subsisted
between the pastor, and this his poor flock; when we reflect on your
conduct in general, and what it has been towards us in particular,
especially as it respected a compensation for your great services, we
have had, and still have reason to conclude that, with the apostle Paul,
it was not our worldly goods that you were looking for, but the good of
our immortal souls, that lay near your heart; and we are made to lament
at the great loss we have already sustained, by your not being able to
dispense the word of life among us as heretofore, and the dreadful
prospect of your making your final leave of us here below, by the call of
the messenger death. But, dear brother, what can we say; the hand of
God is in these things, and we must submit to His will and should not
repine at our loss, if God should please to take you from us, our loss
though great, will we believe, be your eternal gain.

We send this as a testimony of our sincere love to you as a dear
brother and pastor.

Signed by order of the church at a monthly meeting, May 3, 1806.

FREDERICK DOBYNS, Clk.

A letter nearly similar to the above, was written and approved of at
their several church meetings, by the two churches of Happy Creek and
Water Lick, in Frederick and Shenandoah Counties, and signed by their
respective clerks, viz. Charles Buck and Jared Williams, of date nearly
the same as that above.

A few more letters, now in my hands written by individuals to him,
full of expressions of love and high esteem, are for brevity's sake passed
by.

It may not here be amiss to observe, that though Mr. Ireland was
first received into the Separate Baptist connection, yet in the year 1783
(before the union of the then two orders) he joined the Ketocton
Association, as a member of Shenandoah River Church, otherwise called
Upper South River Church.

The following is an extract of a circular letter, written by Mr. Ireland in 1788, by the appointment of the Ketocton Association, to the several churches belonging to that body, and which was approved by the Association.

After stating the general tone of the letters from the churches, the additions to their number of such as it was hoped would be saved, the peace that prevailed in the Association, etc. he proceeded:

> As we are about to take our leave of you, suffer a word of exhortation. Consider dear brethren, He who died for your offences and rose again for your justification, has in some measure entrusted us with a part of His glory here below, and calls upon the world to take notice of us, as the people by whom He expects to be honoured; let us therefore shew to the world the nature of that Spirit we profess to be led and influenced by, adorning the doctrine of God our Saviour in all things, maintaining a life conformable to the gospel of our dear Redeemer. Consider yourselves as strangers and pilgrims on the earth, having no abiding place; be often casting longing looks towards that celestial city, where there is fullness of joy and pleasures for evermore. In the mean time help one another on your way thither, by prayer, counsel and advice; if any are ready to halt, take the road, step in before them, and animate them by your example to follow you as far as you follow Christ. Let unfeigned love to God and one another, possess your breast, and strive to excel in all the virtues of religion.
>
> Be diligent in reading the scriptures, they are able to make you wise unto salvation. Be much in prayer, and diligent in attending the worship of God. Endeavor to keep your children from vice, and from reading vain books. Strengthen the hands of your ministers, who (under Christ) have the care of your souls, etc.

Mr. Ireland was no mean poet. I have heard him say, that in his leisure hours, when he got on a vein of poetry, he could follow it up almost at pleasure. The Rev. Benjamin Ervin, a Presbyterian preacher, of considerable note, and long a resident of Rockingham County Virginia, a man of good natural parts, and who had his education at Princeton College; having been favoured with a pretty lengthy poem of Mr. Ireland's composition, which he highly esteemed; I (some short time after Mr. Ireland's death) presented him with the elegy composed by Mr. Ireland, on the death of Mrs. Ashby, etc. it being then in print.

After reading it deliberately over, he observed that Mr. Ireland was a natural poet. At different periods of his life, he composed a number of poems, but by one means or another, they, at his death, were much scattered, and but few could be come at. It has been said, that Mr. Ireland had lent about sixty of his poems to a friend of his beyond the Allegheny Mountains.

Here follows a few of Mr. Ireland's poems which we presume will be read with pleasure.

For Lucinda Ireland—From her Father July 5, 1800.

1

My little daughter thou may'st see,
A few instructions here for thee
Remember thou art sent to school,
To learn thy book—not play the fool.

2

Obedience to thy master shew,
Respect him—fear him—love him too;
He teaches thee, his rules obey,
By strict observance ev'ry day.

3

If others from their lessons look,
Pay strict attention to thy book.
Thy lesson, strive to get it well,
And ev'ry day thyself excel.

4

If thy school-mates to thee be rude,
Report it not—it is not good,
Use no ill words, that's vain or evil,
Be modest, mannerly and civil.

5

These rules observe, and in them move,
Thou wilt enjoy respect and love,
They'll be to thee, my child, a treasure.
And give thy parents ample pleasure.

1

Has God, the sov'reign God on high,
Appointed once for me to die,
And after death to judgment go,
Their doom to hear for bliss or woe?

2

Will precious souls renew'd by grace,
With the Redeemer have a place,
When ev'ry unregen'rate heart,
Must hear that piercing word depart?

3

Unhappy then my present case,
A stranger both to God and grace,
Yet God in Christ my soul must know,
Or I go down to endless woe.

4

Shew mercy to my soul O God,
O cleanse me with atoning blood,
Thy Son reveal and Spirit grant,
No greater blessings do I want.

5

Then judgment come, I shall not fear,
But with Thy chosen saints appear,
Yet while on earth, I'll spend my days,
As sov'reign grace shall have the praise.

The above was frequently sung by Mr. Ireland and congregation in meeting.

To the tune, Jesus can make a dying bed, etc.

1

How lovely to see blooming youth,
Seek God when in their early days,
Advancing in the path of truth,
Their hearts engaged in His ways.

2

The pleasures that their souls doth find,
When bless'd Jesus is the choice,
Brings sweet content upon the mind,
And fills them with exalted joys.

3

Young people fly to Christ's embrace,
On nothing else but Jesus rest,
Religion, virtue, youth and grace,
What dignity is there possess'd.

4

Refined pleasure you will know;
Pleasure transcending that of sin,
At last you'll to your Jesus go,
Eternally to be with Him.

1

America exult in God
With joyful acclamation,
Who has thro' scenes of war and blood,
Display'd to thee salvation.

When armed hosts
With warlike boasts,
Did threaten thy destruction,
And cross'd the main,
With martial train,
To compass thy subjection.
Thy sole resource was God alone,
Who hear'd thy cries before His throne,
Beheld with hate their schemes of blood,
Impending o'er thee like a flood,
And made them know it was in vain,
To make thee longer drag their chain,
That thou should be
A nation free
From their unjust oppression.

2

Hail now ye sons of liberty,
Behold thy constitution,
Despotic power and tyranny
Have seen their dissolution.
No clattering arms,
No war's alarms,
Nor threats of royal vengeance,
Thy hostile foes,
Has left off those,
Now own thy Independence.
Replete with peace, valiant we stand
Freedom the basis of our land,
Blest with the beams of gospel light,
Our souls emerge from sable night;
Jehovah's heralds loud proclaim,
Eternal life thro' Jesus' name,
Points out His blood,
The way to God,
For our complete salvation.

3

Amidst the blessings we enjoy,
From God the gracious Giver,
Let gratitude our hearts employ,
To praise His name for ever,
Beware of pride,
Lest like a tide,
It flows, and gains, possession;
'Mongst Empires all,
Both great and small,
Pride always brought oppression.
Pride finds the way to rule and reign,
And forges the despotic chain,
Denies we should enjoy or have
The right that God in nature gave;
Against this baleful evil fight,
Resist its force with all your might,
And join as one,
Before the throne,
That God would keep us humble.

4

Most gracious God, we Thee adore,
Whose mercies faileth never,
Thy guardian care we now implore,
Be thou our King for ever.
May gospel rays,
Divinely blaze,
With an immortal lustre,
And teach us how,
Our hearts to bow,
To the Redeemer's sceptre.
O may the silver trump of peace,
Within our Empire never cease,
Until the ransom'd purchas'd race,

Are called in by sov'reign grace,
Then may the conflagration come,
And sinners rise to hear their doom;
Thy chosen ones
In endless songs
Will shout forth hallelujahs.

The following was made in consequence of the death of his little
daughter Letitia, no date inserted.

O RELIGION, HOW AMIABLE ART THOU.
1
How mutable are all things here below,
Subject to change, experience makes me know;
Nothing exists upon this earthly span,
A proper object of the heart of man,
The only center t'fix our all upon,
Is the supreme eternal God alone.

2
Too often are the sons of men propense,
To place their comforts in the things of sense,
Exterior objects they so much revere,
Husbands their wives, parents their children dear,
As if that God designed them to be,
Their only comfort and felicity.

3
But oh! Let death their precious lives arrest,
Uncertain comfort then, they prove at best,
Husbands and wives, each other's loss lament,
Parents their children, from their bosoms rent,
Whilst pregnant sorrow vents itself, and moans
In lamentations, sighs and heavy groans.

4

When I have seen death's rapid conquests spread,
Parents in grief, their present comforts fled,
And all their hopes with them, laid in the grave,
Which if they liv'd, they did expect to have;
To sympathize, my heart would oft' incline,
Yet thankful feel, the stroke was kept from mine.

5

A loving father, I myself, may call,
Felt tender passions for my children all,
Had God designed one of them to take,
Left me the object for to designate,
I should have said, "Since one of them must die,
Lord choose Thyself, a neutral I shall lie."

6

Although I never could myself impeach,
Of want of love unto my children each,
Yet 'mongst them all I had a favourite,
In whom, through fondness, I took much delight,
But always hid my passion from the rest,
That none should know, I loved her the best.

7

By me she always set the greatest store,
Which made my passions to her glow the more,
Her talk was pleasant, and her temper mild,
Artful and witty, though she was a child;
Which made me hope, if she had days to live,
Much satisfaction in her, I should have.

8

Too much she was the object of my love,
Which made me fear, this child a snare would prove,
Engross my heart, then bring me for to rue,

I lov'd the creature, more than 'twas its due;
Whilst conscience often unto me did say,
A sov'reign God will soon take her away.

Note. As these poems were found on separate pieces of paper, mostly without dates, or any arrangement, and some of them only transcripts from the original, it cannot be expected they will follow each other in the order of time in which they were written, and possibly they may not all be so correct.

The following piece is supposed to have been written on the death of an infant of Mr. Thomas Buck's Esqr. who with his wife were members of one of Mr. Ireland's churches.

1

Sweet little babe, what! Art thou gone
Through yonder skies, to us unknown?
Hast thou just open'd to the light,
Then from this stage didst take thy flight?
What, little stranger, didst thou find,
Here so disgustful to thy mind,
That made thee thus resign thy breath
Up to the stroke of cruel death?

2

Hail happy babe! time is no more,
Thy bitter cup of life is o'er;
Temptation and calamity
Are strangers both unknown to thee;
Thou didst but taste and then from those
Withdrew to undisturb'd repose.

3

But hark—I hear the father groan!
The bowels yearn, the mother mourn!
Their throbbing breasts, in great distress,
Crying it's gone, our child, alas
But stop, dear parents, be it known,

Almighty God takes but His own;
Perhaps he saw distress to form,
So hous'd the plant before the storm.

4

Yield to the stroke, let tears be dry,
Since it is crown'd with victory,
Tho' it is gone; and can't return,
To it you'll go, then cease to mourn,
Press for the glories that endure,
Happy eternal life secure;
Then when you both remove from this
You'll meet it in the ports of bliss.

The above was penned by Mr. Ireland at midnight.

AN ELEGY

Composed by the Rev. James Ireland, on the death of his pious friend, Mrs. Peggy Ashby wife of Captain Nathaniel Ashby, of Kentucky, who departed this life, August 2, 1802.

What solemn tidings, am I made to hear,
With painful accents, grating on my ear—
The troubled Bearer, tells with plaintive tone,
Dear Ashby's partner, and my friend is gone!
Unfeeling Death, upon her heart hath trod,
Dismiss'd her Spirit, and sent it to God.

Beloved woman!—many knew thy worth!
And shall I pause? To set thy virtues forth
Can be no crime—though languidly I paint,
The true believer and the pious saint;
Friendship constrains, its pointed voice doth say,

It is a tribute which you ought to pay.

In early youth, though young, her tender mind,
    To ways immortal never was inclin'd;
Her conscience felt conviction's pointed dart,
And Sinai's thunder pierc'd her trembling heart;
    Deeply alarm'd, her soul replete with grief,
    Fled to the law, in hopes to find relief,
    But found performances could not impart
    Relief or peace unto her wounded heart;
    Beheld it just, if God should doom to die,
    Although resolv'd at Jesus' feet to lie;
    In pensive tones, would to herself declare,
    If I must perish, let me perish there.

At length that hour, that happy hour appears,
    Which God designed should allay her fears,
    Relieve her heart, dry up her weeping eyes,
    And make her soul to joyful transports rise.
The great Redeemer, full of truth and grace,
    Is brought to view, adapted to her case;
    In Him she views salvation, life, and peace
    In Him she views a perfect righteousness;
She bears His cheering voice to the distrest,
    "Come heavy laden, I will give you rest;"
    Yields up unto His efficacious call,
    And on Him ventures her eternal all.
Her guilt remov'd her soul is fill'd with peace,
Ascribes the praise to free and sovereign grace.

Nor shall my Muse, in silence not express,
How much she honoured what she did profess,
    With real virtue her whole life was crown'd,
    And spread her fragrancy to all around—
    In her domestic duties, all conjoin'd,
    A wife, a parent—and to servants kind;

Progressing on—in every duty found,
At length affliction shoots the mortal wound;
And while her dear connexions on her gaze,
Her virtues then, shone forth in greater blaze.

A pious friend addressed her and said,
"Of death," dear madam, "Feel you any dread?"
"No," she replies, "I trust on Christ alone,
Therefore, can say, my fear of death is gone;
That precious Jesus, whom I have in view,
Is my sure hope and my salvation too."

Ling'ring she lay—The moment now transpires,
She is resign'd; the pious saint expires;
Attending spirits waft her soul along,
Soaring aloft, she joins the happy throng;
Resplendant beauties now before her roll,
Surrounding glory beams upon her soul;
Her harp is strung; in lofty strains doth sing
Eternal glory to my God and King.
Adieu! Blest spirit! Duty doth me bind,
To speak a word to him thou left behind.
Surviving Ashby; Thy friend bears a part
Of those distresses that affect thy heart!
Distresses, which thyself can best relate;
Afflicted man! I know thy loss is great!
My ears have hear'd, my eyes did often see,
How kind a monitor she was to thee.

My muse refrain—add nothing to his grief,
A soothing friend he wants, can aid relief;
His heart hath felt a piercing scene of woe,
Conflicting passions in his bosom glow—
Bear up, dear sir, resign, no more complain,
What is thy loss, is her eternal gain.

Was she permitted once thy face to see,
In tender strains, would not her language be?
My once dear partner, cease and grieve no more
Thy Peggy's gain'd the blest celestial shore!
Let true Religion be your constant guide,
Let no wrong conduct lead thy feet aside!
At death, God will thy weary soul dismiss,
Transmit it up to everlasting bliss!
Then will I meet you on the eternal shore,
To live in Jesus and to die no more.

Mr. Ireland had, at his death, the following living children; viz. James, Francis, and Thomas, Nancy Jean, and Letty by his first wife, and Lucinda by the second.

Francis married first and died last fall, leaving six children; Thomas married next and is removed to the State of Ohio, has several children; Nancy married Captain Elijah Pollard, who removed to Kentucky, has several children; Jean married Elder Samuel O. Hendren, a Baptist minister, and died about four months after his marriage.

Letty married Mr. Isaac Baker, and they are moved to Kentucky, and have several children. Lucinda married Mr. Alexander Compton, a merchant and Post-master, who lives at a place called Nineveh, in Frederick County Virginia, has four children; James the eldest, and last to marry, is married to a daughter of Mr. Thomas Newels, and has two children living; he lives on his father's old place on a branch of Crooked Run, Frederick County: he is a respectable member of a Baptist Church in his vicinity.

FINIS

Copyright secured according to law.

The History of Rev. Joseph Craig

A History of Rev. Joseph Craig

A sketch of a journal of the Rev. Joseph Craig in which is contained his experience. A sketch of his gospel labor, travels, persecution, sufferings, spiritual and conflicts.

To which is annexed
Prayer and several spiritual songs together with an address to his daughters.
Written by himself,
Lexington, Kentucky

Printed and sold by Thomas Skillman opposite the postoffice, 1813.

Chapter 1

I was born they say in Virginia the 11th day of June in the year of our Lord 1741. My father inclined to the High Church; my mother had some knowledge of the Presbyterian doctrine and often reproved me for my rattling and vain joking. And when I was about eight or ten years old, I was often dreadfully afraid I should be miserable after death and was very desirous to be good. But I never had then heard the way of salvation by Christ, as there were only about five or six Baptists within thirty or forty miles and no others that preached Him aright. So I lived until I was married and got to be three and twenty years old.

All this time did I live (for thirteen or fourteen years) under a sense of condemnation. I was most sensible of this in the time of lightning and thunder. I used to pray often, most commonly when I was in my bed: but, when it thundered hard, I was often on my knees, saying over all the prayers I knew, again and again till the thunder was past. My fears were great, that if I died before I was better, I should be lost from God forever. So I continued till one man rode to the gap where I lived and told me, if I would go and hear the Baptist they would tell me something I would like, he did believe; and some such talk. And when he went off, I felt very awful and strange that I could scarcely walk! After some time the preacher came and had an appointment to preach at night. I went to hear him, but nothing seemed to affect me. At length, two persons were talking together—one said to the other, the prayerbook was not scripture. That word seemed as if it destroyed or took away half my religion, and left me standing on I knew not what. After some time, the preacher came again and preached several times. I followed him down about twenty miles. He preached in an old house. I had been with him and his company several days, and felt, by this time, a strong love for them; and while he preached, I stood near him, and gave all attention. After he had done, we returned toward our homes. On my way, I felt some solemn and awful impressions on my mind; those impressions I feared to lose, I wished to say nothing to any one, but kept praying to myself. When I got home, I stood in the yard and seemed rather afraid to go in.

My wife saw me and shed tears, and said some things ailed me. The next morning the case seemed plain: It seemed as though the glory of God appeared to me, and in me; and I could see the Lord in me, and I in Him (by faith); and that I was safe and happy and clothed with His glorious, all sufficient righteousness. Now I felt so safe, as though I was taken out of hell into heaven.

I almost thought God showed me my relations and near friends in the broad road to death and hell. I talked to them. Some heard me and said I was right; and some did not like it at all. I had little thought God would speak by me; I preached in a private way to all I got a chance to speak to; but particularly to our Parson. He got angry at me and raised his fist at me and said he was the maddest man I ever saw when he was mad! So I persuaded three of my brothers to go about forty miles with me to the meeting, to hear Brother Thomas[23] preach.

They seemed fully to fall in with the doctrine which he preached, but none of them professed conversion at that time so we returned home.

---

[23] Craig may be referring to David Thomas, a well respected Baptist minister\revivalist who labored extensively in northern Virginia. See Taylor, *Lives of Virginia Baptist Preachers*, 41-44.

Chapter 2

It seemed to me from the first of my conviction, that God had something for me to do in the preaching work. Though I knew it not; yet I preached in a private way to all with whom I had an opportunity of conversing, I went twice to the Parson, and to my father's family; and I often expostulated with my neighbors when I chanced to meet them, as I was the first one who professed conversion among them. But after I had a great feeling sense of pardon and the Lord's love manifested to me. I got to moving and fell into great darkness for some months. At length, being at Brother Waller's meeting the magistrates were ordering to prison, and Brother Chiles was exhorting near them.[24] I was praying the power of God came on me, and it seemed to me, drove from my heart all sin and darkness, and my love to God seemed plainer and stronger than ever. And this scripture was immediately applied to me: "Now you are clean through the word I have spoken to you" (John 15:3). And might I say, with the Apostle, "Perfect love casteth out all fear" (I John 4:18). I prayed God aloud for sometime. It seemed as if I never got so low and full of unbelief again. Under my time coldness and darkness, my preaching seemed to be but little blessed, but now being quickened again, I was enabled to go on my way rejoicing.

I traveled with Brother Lewis and Brother Chiles. Chiles said I was to him as Titus was to Paul. About this time, Brother Waller was chosen to travel through churches for one year, and he chose me to travel with him. We traveled great part of the year over the great mountains, and down on the bay side; and the brethren by their language and private conversations owned me as his help-mate, which confirmed me in the faith and belief that God had sent me to help him. When I stayed at

---

[24] Waller and Chiles are likely John Waller and James Chiles. Both men preached extensively in northern Virginia and Waller may well have been the most persecuted Baptist preacher in the late eighteenth century. See Little, *Imprisoned Preachers and Religious Liberty in Virginia*, passim, as well as Taylor, *Lives of Virginia Baptist Preachers*, 77-84.

home some weeks, I felt coldness, darkness, and deadness: but when I got out from home two or three days, it seemed plain to me that I had left all and followed the Lord.

Chapter 3

The journey of Brother Waller and myself, as his assistant, over the great mountains.

As we lived in Virginia, below the great mountains, our journey over two ridges and back would be two hundred miles, the way we went.

After we got over the Blue Ridge, as it was called, we sat on the bank of the river Shenandoah, while Brother Samuel Harris administered the Lord's Supper to about one hundred communicants. After which Waller and myself went up between the river and said mountains about thirty miles, with a brother preacher (by the name of Coons)[25] where we were invited to dine. We went in and before we were done dinner, Brother Coons said, "These brothers thought to get horses of thee, to go over to Smith's Creek, to do some business there."

Brother Mocks[26] said he was hauling stone, I observed, that we thought to have forgotten horses would carry us. After awhile, we went out, and he had saddled his horses, and said we might ride them. We got to the church, and stayed part of two days, and ordained one Elder and preached, and came back to the white house, near where Brother Mocks lived. He met us there. One or both of our horses he had shod, and in his hand he had a dollar. He said one sister told him to give us that and

---

[25] Brother Coons is probably John Koontz. See Taylor, *Lives of Virginia Baptist Ministers*, pp. 96-101.
[26] It is difficult to say with certainty but Brother Mocks may be John Marks. See Little, *Imprisoned Preachers and Religious Liberty in Virginia*, p. 26.

we must cut it in two between us, and desired it might not be known who she was!

We never said a word about living by the gospel; but, in private, the brethren would sometimes contribute a small sum, amounting to about one shilling a day, while we were out and sometimes none. When we got back to the white house, we examined who was the minister there; but, as the church was divided between Brother Coons and Brother Murfit,[27] we could ordain none, according to our customary rule; but baptized four persons. We commended in a large upper room, prepared for meeting by one Coffmon,[28] who had built it for that purpose. We had a happy time there, and much love and union appeared among us during the time of our meeting.

When we were set off, one young woman said, weeping, she wished she had never seen these men. She added she should never see them again, which was the cause of her weeping. The night we stayed there, Brother Waller said he had no objection against traveling with me, but I would not let him sleep. After leaving this place, we found in our bag, a first-rate large cake, and we were traveling along, about twenty of us, eating the large cake. We lay that night at a Dutchman's. We left there the next day, and crossed the Blue Ridge at Milian's Path—we were told it was seven miles to the top—nearly half that seven miles was so steep that it was very hard to ride; and when we got on the top, the trees were not much larger than apple trees, and the air was quite strong. And here it was that Brother Waller composed a spiritual song. That night we got down on the head waters of the Rappahannock, to one Brother Joel Earley's, where we preached, washed feet. The rich Earley stood near the door. Then we parted, full of love, and peace and joy, in believing. And Brother Waller said, before that fire died, he composed another

---

[27] Brother Murfit may be Anderson Moffett. See Little, *Imprisoned Preachers*, pp. 428-434.

[28] Brother Coffman is probably Martin Kaufman who converted under John Picket's and Lewis Craig's ministry. Kaufman once received a beating after being mistaken for John Koontz. See Garnett Ryland, *The Baptists of Virginia, 1699-1926* (Richmond: The Virginia Baptist Board of Missions and Education, 1955), pp. 56, 58.

spiritual song, the first line of which is, "Come let us take an humble view."

Here the songs both follow—first, the one composed on the mountain by Brother Waller.

Let me but hear my lovely Saviour
Bid me comfort His lovely spouse;
Saying, she is dear to me, I'll have her,
Though wicked men and hell oppose.

The blessed message, so transporting,
O! I would run to Zion's door.
And knock and sound a loud salvation
To the half-starv'd hungry poor.

The flock of Jesus, how I'd feed them.
In pleasant groves, there they should rest;
Into fat pastures I would lead them,
To lean upon their Shepherd's breast.

There I would leave them with my Master,
And should His Spirit bid me go.
Over a mountain or deep river,
I'd run and let poor sinners know.

I'd baptize every faithful follower,
Who did repent and did believe,
Who did resolve to be a soldier
Of Jesus Christ and Him to serve.

The greatest profit, prince, or honor,
That after all I'd wish to have,
Should be to serve my Lord and Master,
'Till I'm committed to my grave.

Waller's Second Song.

Come let us take a humble view
Of Jesus Christ, our dearest Friend,
When going to the place He knew
The wicked Jews His life would end.
Hosannah to the loving Lamb of God,
Who brought poor sinners with His most
             precious blood.

Most steadfastly His head He set,
     Toward Jerusalem to go;
Resolv'd to pay our dreadful debt,
And take on Him the curse of sinner's law, Hosannah,

The Scribes, the Pharisees, and Priests,
Resolv'd to stop our dear Lord's breath,
Barrabas, they chose to be releas'd,
While their sport was to see Christ's death.
        Hosannah,

On Him a crown of thorns they put,
And smote thereon with reed and staff:
Blindfolding Him, His cheeks they cuff't,
Then ask'd Him who did smite the last.
        Hosannah,

In token of mock-majesty,
With purple robes then He was drest;
Saying, "Hail, King," they bow'd the knee,
Then, with His cross, His shoulder prest.
        Hosannah,

His cross up Calvary's Mount He bore,
Then being stript, thereon was laid;
His hands and feet were nailed through,

And fastened to the fatal wood.
Hosannah,

Then, reared up betwixt two thieves,
Three hours hung in bitter pain,
'Till, with loud cries, death, Him releas'd,
From all that wreck He so complain'd,
Hosannah,

The sufferings which His body bore,
Were trifling when compar'd to those;
The hiding of His Father's face,
When time shall end, the saints shall know.
Hosannah,

Two Jewish rulers did inter
Our dearest Lord in a new tomb,
Where He did sleep 'till the third day,
Then rose to heaven, His native home.
Hosannah,

Sinners, behold your sacrifice,
See all your sins upon the cross:
Believe and sing redeeming love,
And give the Lord of life your praise.
Hosannah to the loving Lamb of God,
Who brought poor sinners with His most
precious blood.

Chapter 4

As to my travels and standing with Brother Joseph Bledsoe.

Brother Bledsoe made a covenant with me, that if I would stand with him in society, should be sure to equal with him in the work of the ministry, and have every liberty which he had in society; which he was faithful to perform to me. In this society I stood, and I went about eight or nine times with him to the Essex meeting, about sixty miles off, in one year. As Brother Bledsoe had the care of a church in Essex, and Brother Lewis the care of one in Spotsylvania, the persecution in Caroline was great—Where I[29] was taken four times (by the civil officer) for preaching without legal license, as they called it, i.e. from the High Church of England. This was the common complaint. Once they put me in the criminal jail, where I sang about one hour, exceedingly happy—After which, they let me have the bounds, on bail. While I was there, I seemed as if I had said, "Lord, I have left all and followed Thee," and "proved my faith by my work"—and it seemed as if He had said, face-to-face, "I can believe you have." After I had stayed about three weeks there, I went to the outer part of the bounds, and sat down: and it seemed that, if I would but look up, I should see the glory of God. Then I seemed near home! I said, with tears, "Lord, why cannot I follow Thee now?"

---

[29] Craig's note in the text: Read – Matthew 5:10-14, 45: "Blessed are they which are persecuted for righteousness's sake: for theirs is the kingdom of heaven. Blessed are ye when men shall revile you, and persecute you, and shall say all manners of evil against you falsely for my sake. Rejoice, and be exceeding glad; for great is your reward in heaven: for so persecuted they the prophets which were before you." But I tried to obey the 44th verse of this chapter: "But I say unto you, Love your enemies, bless them that curse you, do good to them that hate you, and pray for them which despitefully use you and persecute you." Here follows the 45th verse, as a reason for doing: "That ye may be the children of your Father which is in heaven: for He maketh His sun to rise on the evil and on the good, and sendeth rain on the just and the unjust." O Persecution! what hath thou done? In ages past and gone?

One time, I had preached, and after I had done, the constable took hold of me, and said I must go with him. I thought God did not send me to prison; and if Satan did, I would not go before T --. That warrant said, "He should bring me before him or some other magistrate in the country." I would go before Mr. H --. I thought the Lord let me know the prince of this world cometh. One man said, "Come, go away." The constable had then let me go. I said to the man, you must go with me. We went out at the other door—someone shut the door by the house stable. The constable thought I was in the house but I was gone out at the other door, and into the woods. T—and his company came and hunted the closets and rooms but found me not.

I had an appointment for meeting next day below, in my way to Essex; and when I got there, I thought, if war was fashionable, that I would try and war a good warfare; and, as I had gotten into it, I did not care how much I suffered for the Lord's sake; and I concluded, that they might do their worst, and I would try and do what I could for the Lord. And surely I did cry aloud that day! And we had a good time. And, on another day, I was at meeting in the same county, and had been speaking (or preaching.)

The constable came, and some big men with him. He came round the company, and took hold of me. I asked him to let me get done the hymn which we were singing. He stood and held me by the arm. He then led me along the way, to carry me to prison. The congregation were all moved along—some began to exhort the constable to take care what he did; and then some of the congregation did praise the Lord aloud! They led me, about three miles, to T --, and sat with me awhile; and then they went away. At dusk I was conducted into an upper chamber, and they took my four-penny knife from me, for fear I would kill some of them! I slept but little that night. In the morning the constable and company were in the porch, talking. As I was in the hall, and other room, I thought they had forgotten me—I might, perhaps, go away. I went out of their sight—they did not mind me—I feared to be my own jailor—I would try to go off—I could run to meeting better than home—I thought I would try to get off from among them—I got about fifty yards, and one gave an alarm, "Craig is gone."

In one minute a gang of men, some on horseback, and a gang of dogs, of different sizes, were after me. I thought they should catch me, if they could; but, if they did, they should have a race for it. I ran steadily on, and got into the woods; but the dogs followed me true—I tried to dodge them, but in vain—I spoke to them, but had to stop; they would give no quarters. The men came up and one of them took me by the hair, and raised his fist to strike me; but his companion caught his hand. They led me to the house, and commanded me to prison. I got on my horse, with one brother behind me. I said I must keep my conscience clear, or I should fall into keen despair—I did not care about life or death. The man behind me said I should do as I pleased. I got out at the gate, alighted down from my horse, and stood still. The constable asked what ailed me—was sullen? I told him I would have no hand in carrying Joseph Craig to prison. He then came and sat me on my horse; his companion came with a rope, and tied my feet together under my horse, which hurt me considerably; and he took hold of the bridle, and led my horse almost ten miles. Being now near the prison, the rope being stiff, untied, and I thought the Lord let me know I was free—so I observed to the constable, do you not remember, "Pilate took water and washed his hands, and said he was clear of the blood of that just Person?" He said he did. I told him he was now carrying me to prison—that I had a wife and children to take care of. He said he would not do anything to hurt me, but only to clear himself of the law. So when we got to the prison, he put me in, but the door would not lock—so that night I sat off toward home; and so got clear of them for that time &c. &c. &c.

Chapter 5

An account of my journey to Essex County, in the first big snow, with Brother Bledsoe, as he then had the care of the church there, and chose me to help him.

After we had been there one or two days, it began to snow, and snowed and hailed part of several days (perhaps about four days). In the meantime, we had meeting, and several got converted, as we supposed, and believed, before we sat off for home!

Brother Bledsoe had about forty miles home, and I about sixty. By the help of some roads being broken open, we got about fifteen miles the first day; and the second day, we had about twenty-five miles to Brother Bledsoe's; and, by the help of a great road being trodden open, we got to Brother Bledsoe's about midnight. As my clothes were but thin, I got hurt some from the frost; for the weather was nearly as cold as I ever felt, and for about eight miles before we got to Brother Bledsoe's, we had no road nor a trace. The snow was about one foot and a half deep, and our horses often fell on the snow, but through much suffering, we got to Brother Bledsoe's about midnight. Then I had better than twenty miles home. I got off early the next morning, and drove hard all day, being extremely anxious to get home; but did not make it out that night. I got within about six miles of home, and had to stay all night at a very poor man's house. I hurried off very early in the morning. After going about two miles on the track toward Brother John's, his mill boys had trodden the track open, which my horse would follow, bleeding very much about the feet; but would not go the way I wanted him to go. Brother John lent me a low horse. In going from thence to my house, he would fall on the snow, and spattered the blood on the snow with his feet. And when I got home, I found that my wife had suffered from firewood, and about half of my hogs had frozen to death in the woods. One or two of my children did not know me, and called me the man. So I got home that time, &c.

B 2

Chapter 6

An account of my journey to Richmond County, with the Rev. Joseph Bledsoe.—The distance was about seventy miles from my house.

Said Bledsoe had chosen me to go with him, and help him in the way of preaching. I attended meeting with him eight times in one year, about sixty or seventy miles off. At a certain time, we had meeting in Essex.—Some young people came to our meeting about eight miles by land, and two miles by water, across the Rappahannock River. As they took so much pains in coming so far by land and water, we promised to go over and see them. We went and had meeting day and night. In the night, the Lord seemed to bless us greatly with His blessed power and presence; and, as I was exhorted, I observed to the people, if I could not so much love, and the Lord would continue to bless me as He had on the present occasion, that I would come to see them, if I had to throw the water out of the boat with my hat, little thinking I was so near danger. We had to cross back in an old boat, that was very leaky, and when we left the land, the river did not seem very rough; but when we got a mile from shore, the water beat very much into the boat. I sat with a piece of gourd throwing out water. And when Brother Bledsoe spoke, it seemed as if his faith was so strong, that the boat would not sink. But when the owner of the boat spoke, he was so scared, it seemed as if we should sink notwithstanding all our efforts to prevent it. When we got on shore, we all knelled down, and thanked God for our having escaped the deep. There was in the water a large shoal of porpoises, very much like resembling black hogs. After this we immediately returned home, about the year 1775.

Chapter 7

A Prayer, by said Craig.

Almighty, great and eternal God, we desire to be always looking up to Thy glorious Majesty for every blessing—for time and for eternity. We desire to thank Thee for all the good things Thou hast given us, of temporal and spiritual things; that is to say, Thy written word, Thine own sent ministers and ordinances, and the company and fellowship of Thy children, and all the means of Thy gospel. For sending Thy blessed Spirit to apply the redemption bought with blood! Lord, we thank Thee for all the work of that blessed Spirit on us and in us. And still we are beggars, and we pray that Thou wouldest increase our faith. Lord we pray give us of Thy living bread to eat which came down from heaven; and to drink of that water of life freely, that came out of the throne of God and of the Lamb. O Lord, come unto us, and reveal Thy love in us, and let us taste and see Thou art our Lord and our God.

O! give us perfect love, that casteth out all fear.

O! satisfy our souls by giving us abundance of Thy love. O! satisfy us that Thou art our Saviour and Comforter, by giving us strong consolation in our hearts. Yea, Lord, satisfy our souls that Thou art our Saviour, and portion, and Comforter; and that Thou wilt deliver us from every evil work, and bring us to Thy glorious kingdom. Amen.

Once as I returned from a meeting in Essex County, I composed the following spiritual song:

> Seven long years I've been a ranging
> Up and down Virginia land,
> Seeking a bride for me Lord Jesus,
> Hoping her love I should obtain.

Long time have I greatly desired
Her joyful favour to obtain;
For which I have gone through all weather,
Both hot, and day, and cold, and rain.

Through frost, and snow, and frightful rivers,
Hunger and thirst, and wicked hands,
Through midnight air, in lonesome places,
Which often caus'd my heart to ache.

All this is but as a small trifle,
If I could but her love obtain,
And I enjoy her love and favour,
Thus would my love and joy be full.

Sometimes I got into her favour,
Her heart and affections almost won;
But Satan, a wise and great opposer,
My joyful heart he caus'd to mourn.

O! might I ever be so happy
To hear my Saviour's bride to say,
Thou art my shepherd, he did send thee
For to guide me along the way.

Such declarations of her favour,
And good witnesses of her love,
Would satisfy my soul's desire,
And my full satisfaction prove.

Long time have I greatly desired
Her joyful favour to obtain;
And, if I'm ever counted worthy,
I'll mind not heat, nor cold nor pain.

Another, by the same

O come, dearest friends, let us follow Jesus,
Surely it is He alone that can relieve us;
But, O! consider well how hard to get to heaven.
Of the twelve that follow'd long, there were sav'd but eleven.

O! loving Lamb of God, who would not Thee follow,
Although it so searing is, and all looks like sorrow,
Yet, if our love is true, it will be a blessed story,
The more we suffer here, the greater will be our glory.

But, O! consider well how hard to follow Jesus,
And, if we follow true, many there will leave us;
And if we are call'd to die, then go and leave us.

Lord, grant us faith and love to bear us safe to Heaven,
There to live and reign with Jesus and the eleven;
They that now cowards prove, and, ere long, turn deserters,
When we in heaven reign, shall not there reign with us.

Do not you hear of war, and of a dreadful rumor?
Our dearest Lord has said it's a token of the summer;
Let us all follow on, let none turn our deserters,
Jesus has gone before, let us follow after.

But, O! how hard it is to part with our acquaintance,
And for us to bid adieu to near and dear relations;
Yet, Lord, at Thy command, we will cheerfully go forward,
Counting not our lives our own, but only just borrowed.

On the road from Bardstown to Frankfort, Ky., after nine days meeting
with Brother Shelton, I composed as follows:

Lord, pity a poor soldier, now in his feeble days,
And take him home to glory, or keep him in Thy ways;

Half three-score years and better a soldier I have been,
O! take me home, dear Jesus, or keep me from all sin.

My faith it is so slender, me courage weak and small,
If Jesus He should call me, I should be at His call,
Where the angels join in battle, and the cherubs swiftly fly,
And the silver trumpet sounding loud, which makes the rebels fly.

If thou shouldst chance to take me home, 'twould be a glorious day,
Old Lucifer his fiery darts no more on me would play;
Twice fifteen years and better a soldier I have been,
Now take me home, dear Jesus, and let me not be slain.

For nine long days and better in battle I have been,
And Jesus' word and Spirit have have spoken my conscience clean;
Now take me home, dear Jesus, and do not from me go,
For to leave me bear [here?] behind Thee, in sorrow, grief, and woe.
A thousand times and better in battle I have been,
Now take me home, hear, dear Jesus, and let me not be slain.

But, still, if Thou deny me, and say that I shall stand,
And face the powers of darkness that rise from hell and land;
This weakness, pain, and sorrow, I'll never mind at all,
If Thy right hand uphold me, and make me conquer all.

Another, by the same Joseph Craig

The daughter of a William Woods professed to get religion at one of our
meeting, amidst much persecution, and desired me to compose a song
on the occasion; which I did as follows:
Come all you saints and angels near, Halle Hallelujah
Come, listen a while, and you shall hear, Halle Hallelujah
A wonder of Almighty grace, Halle Hallelujah
Who set me to sing His praise, sing glory Hallelujah.

My father he did love the Lord Halle &c

And teach and preach His holy word Halle &c
Mother and granny loved the same Halle &c
But my poor soul did dead remain Halle &c

I heard of Jesus many say Halle &c
Could move a sinner's sins away Halle &c
But where to find Him I did not know, Halle &c
Or how to meet with Him below Halle &c

My flesh did war against my soul Halle &c
The night were dark, and very cold Halle &c
The meeting saints I could not slight Halle &c
But sought their Jesus day and night Halle &c

The scandal of the cross I see, Halle &c
That scandal that would fall on me Halle &c
But still I thought I did behold, Halle &c
I wanted Jesus more than gold, Halle &c

I laid me down to take my rest Halle &c
Bemoaning of my dreadful case Halle &c
I thought I could for mercy wait Halle &c
And then I feared I'd come too late Halle &c

I little thought he'd been so nigh, Halle &c
His speaking made me glad and cry Halle &c
He said, "I'm come to thee, my love," Halle &c
"I have a place for thee above" Halle &c

This glorious news I did believe, Halle &c
My sins and sorrows did me leave Halle &c
My soul enraptured in His love Halle &c
I have a place for the above sing glory Hallelujah

Another composed on the death of my daughter, a year old

Friends of the Lord, I pray draw near
Come, think of something new;
Have faith in God, and now come hear
Of what the Lord can do.

When I return'd from work aboard [abroad?],
In my dear Master's field
My daughter dear, ag'd about one year,
I found by death was seiz'd

What sorrow then my heart did fill,
Fear came on every side
For oft I fear'd of such as she
In heaven would few reside.

We cried to Jesus, our dear Friend
With tears, both night and day;
That He would satisfy our souls,
If she was called away.

But death he would not be deni'd,
That we did plainly see;
And that her soul to heaven or hell;
Immediately must flee.

Now, in the time of great distress,
When such near friends must part,
The glory of the Lord come down,
I felt it in my heart.

It came as if I heard Him say,
"Fear not, I am with thee;
I'll satisfy your souls, and shine
Shall go along with me."

Her soul to Christ we freely gave
And, parting, freely bear
Her body to the peaceful grave
'Till Jesus shall appear.

Another, by the same:

Come, all young men, of every degree,
Do you ever think of eternity?
Eternity you all know very well
Your soul it must be in heaven or hell.

Eternity, I will dare to presume
Without you repent, it will be your doom
Down, down to the damned, in wicked estate
O there you'll repent when it is too late.

O sin, O O sin, I know very well,
It led me, in darkness, to the brink of hell;
Until sweet Jesus did open my eyes.
And there I stood wondering in great surprise

O where could I go, or where could I run,
For I could not answer for what I had done;
All prayers and tears I know very well,
Without an interest in Jesus could not save me from hell.

O Jesus, my Saviour, I fall on Thy breast,
If Thou shouldest now damn me I know it is just;
O mercy, O mercy, dear Jesus I cry,
I pardon my guilt, or else I shall die.

O I have had part of all kind of sin
The worst creatures I think I have been;
I never delighted in any of God's ways,
I want to beman [bemoan?] it the rest of my days.

Come all you young men, and think of your souls
Do you all serve God, before you get old;
O cease to do evil, and learn to do well,
And then God will bless you and keep you from hell.

Chapter 8

An account of my life from September 1811 until the sixteenth of
August 1812.

I came home near the last of September 1811 very sore, with ring-
worms over great part of my body and limbs. I had a burning pain and
sickness in my breast; which held me the fall, and winter, and spring.
My sores in the winter were so bad, that many a night I thought I
should die before day. During these severe afflictions of body, I had in
addition thereto, very severe conflicts of the mind, accompanied with
doubts and fears, whether I was a Christian or no.

But when summer came on, my sores mostly cured up; But still a
burning sickness in my breast continued, so as to make me think I
should die in a few days. On the 16th of August, I bless God, I got to
believe that all would work for my good. For the most part of this
month, the Lord seems to be good, and kind, and gracious to me, and
sent His Comforter to abide, I believe, with me, and in me, so as to
make me want to depart, and be with Christ, which is far better. And
for the most part of these two weeks past, He gave me to feel His love
in me, as evidently as I felt the food I ate, glory, power, thanks, love,
and obedience be given to Him, for He is worthy to receive endless
praise. August 17th I fell weak, feeble, and sickly; but thank the blessed

Lord my faith is strong in "Him who made the worlds"—that He is my position, and that He will take care of me, and bring me to His kingdom and Glory (Amen). I was going to die, and I felt as if the Lord would save my soul if I did die.

Chapter 9

February 12, 1813

I have been sick in all about eighteen months. Last August I was very ill indeed. I thought God had given me faith, and a sense of pardoning love, and I was going to His rest.

One told me I was not like to die then—I felt sorry. In my sickness, I thought I felt the sorrows of hell. Often dead, sick about my heart, and often bordering on despair and often hoping for mercy, and thinking "we are saved by hope," and "if we hope for what we see not, then do we wait patiently for it" (Rom. 8:24). I have traveled on till the 12th of February, 1813. These sorrows all to work for my good. My temptations seem to make me seek for the Good Shepherd. My sickness, pains and miseries, killed me to time things, and caused me to seek a better country. Now February 12th, 1813. I have been sick about six weeks this spell; and last night talking to a friend, after some small comfort all day, the Lord was pleased abundantly to satisfy my soul.

But how did my heart melt and tear flow; I thought all I asked the blessed Lord for my life was a full, assurance; which He gave me—an assurance of His love, and grace, and favor (a full manifestation), which He gave me, to my soul's satisfaction. Now I thought I would not fear to meet death, nor the miseries of death. It seemed as if He said, "Your day's work will do for me; I will receive it for a day's work will do for several month before the eleventh day of this month." I said, "If it please Thee, Lord, give me a full manifestation of Thy grace." And if it would please the Lord to I would willingly lay down my life. Having so give me a full manifestation and feeling of His love, many doubts about my salvation—having a heavy heart and sickness therewith. But, as I talked with one about midnight, the eleventh day, it pleases God to reveal His goodness to my soul: I was filled with His love, O! what joy flowed into my heart. My heart seemed to melt and my tears did flow and I did rejoice unspeakably. This 13th I feel the same and have continued to feel that love mostly ever since believing. I am safe and happy and that my salvation seems quite sure and safe, which makes me rejoice. As I often said for forty-seven years past, if I won this race, I was eternally made. My dear brethren believe about this unspeakable goodness to poor me. I thought I was done with this world, and time things. I said, with joy, come death and welcome; I believe I had a great desire to depart and be with the Lord.

Chapter 10

February 15th, 1813

It is thirty-one years since I came to Kentucky. I have sold corn every year in general. I think, about one-hundred barrels in each year. I had thirty or forty thousand acres of land surveyed, and chapped around great parts of it myself and I have no law about any of it, nor do I owe a dollar in the world as I know of. I have raised ten sons and daughters, and given them some learning, and some property towards keeping house: And in all this I have tried to act to the glory of God. Have I fought a fight? In which time I have sinned often, but not willingly or willfully but as my sinful nature caused me to do. But bless God I feel a free pardon of all them and divine life and love flow through my heart—believing to my soul's satisfaction, He loves me. In forty-seven years, I seldom neglected kneeling on my knees, and praying to the Almighty God for His blessing and care.

This I only count, as a proof of my faith in the Lord.

Chapter 11

Being an address to my daughters.

My dear Daughters

I have been troubled much about your souls. The Lord has given me to know a great deal of His goodness and severity—of His ways and doings with the children of men. I have felt much of the effects of both heaven and hell. Once when I was sick, I was near despair—the sorrows of hell seemed to be on me: and when the Lord of late and other times, revealed His love to me it was a taste of heaven. Thus I have had a great sight of heaven and hell. Now my very dear daughters, you are welcome when a sinner dies the devil or some of his angels comes for him and death and hell comes with him. Now my very dear daughters to heaven and Christ and if you love Him, He will love you and reveal His love and glory to you. But if you slight Him, He will slight you, and behave as one jealous toward you, and often cross you.

O my very dear daughters, take my counsel, and when good meetings are about, go to them, and get your hearts empty of the things of this life, till you can, [say?] "Lord, I have left all and follow Thee," as Peter once said (Luke 18:28). O my dear seek the Lord while He may be found, and call upon Him while He is near. O mind His promises in the Testament.

Pray without ceasing when you stand, where you lie, sit or go, pray, "Lord help me." Take my councel [counsel?] my dear, and don't [stop?]

until you find His love in your hearts. Farewell—and you will fare well if you find Him "of whom Moses and the Prophets did write" (John 1:45). Joseph Craig.

Appendix

How Some Baptists Were Persecuted

Adapted from Lewis Peyton Little, *Imprisoned Preachers and Religious Liberty in Virginia*

Name	County	Incident
Afferman, John	Middlesex	Cruelly beaten—incapacitated for work.
Alderson, John	Botetourt	Jailed for (?).
Ammon, Thomas	Culpeper	Jailed for preaching.
Anthony, Joseph	Chesterfield	Jailed for preaching. "Three months."
Baker, Elijah	Accomac	Pelted with apples and stones.
Baker, Elijah	Accomac	Banishment attempted.
Baker, Elijah	Accomac	Jailed for preaching. Fifty-six days.
Banks, Adam	Culpeper	Jailed for (?).
Barrow, David	Nansemond	Ducked and nearly drowned by 20 men.
Barrow, David	Nansemond	Dragged from the house and driven away.
Burrus, John	Caroline	Jailed for preaching.
Chambers, Thomas	Orange	Jailed for (?).
Chastain, Rane	Chesterfield	Ordered to leave the county, or go to jail.
Chastain, Rane	Chesterfield	Commanded to take a dram, or be whipped.
Chiles, James	Spotsylvania	Jailed for preaching.

		"Forty-three days."
Choning, Bartholomew	Caroline	Jailed for (?).
Clay, Eleazer	Chesterfield	Man rode up to cowhide him—failed.
Clay, John	(?)	Jailed for preaching.
Corbley, John	Culpeper	Frequently taken from pulpit—beaten.
Corbley, John	Orange	Jailed for preaching.
Corbley, John	Culpeper	Jailed for preaching.
Craig. Elijah	Culpeper	Jailed for preaching. "One Month."
Craig, Elijah	Culpeper	Jailed for preaching. Duration unknown.
Craig, Elijah	Orange	Jailed for preaching. Seventeen or 18 days.
Craig, Elijah	Orange	Jailed for preaching. "A considerable time."
Craig, Joseph	Spotsylvania	Apprehended, but escaped.
Craig, Joseph	Orange	Presented for being absent from church.
Craig, Lewis	Spotsylvania	Indicted, tried, but not imprisoned.
Craig, Lewis	Spotsylvania	Jailed for preaching. "Four weeks."
Craig, Lewis	Caroline	Arrested and required to give bond.
Craig, Lewis	Caroline	Jailed for preaching. "Three months."
Craig, Lewis	Caroline	Carried to Williamsburg on habeas corpus.
Delaney, John	Culpeper	Jailed for permitting a man to pray.
Eastin, Augustine	Chesterfield	Jailed for preaching.
Elkins, Richard	Pittsylvania	Two men started for warrant. Frightened.
Falkner, Richard	Middlesex	Arrested but released.
Fristoe, Daniel	Fauquier	Service interrupted by curses and silly antics.
Fristoe, Daniel	Stafford	Warrant issued but not executed.

Fristoe, Daniel	Stafford	Gun presented to his breast.
Fristoe, William	Stafford	Application for warrant for him refused.
Fristoe, William	Stafford	Pursued by man with gun, but escaped.
Fristoe, William	Stafford	Taken by a warrant, went to Philadelphia.
Goolrich, James	Caroline	Jailed for preaching.
Greenwood, James	Middlesex	Presented for being absent from church.
Greenwood, James	King and Queen	Jailed for preaching. "Sixteen days."
Greenwood, James	Middlesex	Jailed for preaching. "Forty-six days."
Hargate, Thomas	Amherst	Jailed for preaching.
Harriss, Samuel	Pittsylvania	Mightily opposed and slandered.
Harriss, Samuel	Culpeper	"You shall not preach here."
Harriss, Samuel	Culpeper	Meeting broken up by a mob.
Harriss, Samuel	N. Carolina	Knocked down while preaching.
Harriss, Samuel	Culpeper	Door battered down.
Harriss, Samuel	Culpeper	Arrested as a vagabond, schismatic, etc.
Harriss, Samuel	Orange	Pulled down and hauled about by hair, hand, etc.
Harriss, Samuel	Loudon	Locked up in gaol for some time.
Herndon, Edward	Caroline	Jailed for preaching.
Ireland, James	Culpeper	Tried to suffocate him with smoke.
Ireland, James	Culpeper	Tried to blow him up.
Ireland, James	Culpeper	Tried to poison him.
Ireland, James	Culpeper	Injured for life.
Ireland, James	Culpeper	Drunken rowdies put in same cell with him.
Ireland, James	Culpeper	Threatened with public whipping.

Ireland, James	Culpeper	horses ridden over his hearers at jail;
Ireland, James	Culpeper	Men made their water in his face.
Ireland, James	Culpeper	Jailed for preaching. Five months.
Ireland, James	(?)	Opposition everywhere.
Kaufman, Martin	Shenandoah	Severely beaten with a stick.
Koontz, John	Shenandoah	Severely beaten with butt end of large cane.
Koontz, John	(?)	Met in the road and beaten.
Koontz, John	(?)	Arrested and started to jail, but released.
Lane, Dutton	Lunenburg	"Charged not to come there again."
Lane, Dutton	Pittsylvania	Endured much persecution.
Lane, Dutton	Pittsylvania	His mother beaten by his father.
Leland, John	Orange	Threatened with a gun.
Lewis, Ivison	Gloucester	"Met with violent opposition."
Lewis, Ivison	Essex	Arrested but not imprisoned.
Lovall, William	King and Queen	Jailed for preaching. "Sixteen days."
Lunsford, Lewis	Lancaster	
Lunsford, Lewis	Northumberland	His preaching interrupted by mob violence and legal proscription.
Lunsford, Lewis	Richmond	
Lunsford, Lewis	Westmoreland	
Lunsford, Lewis	Richmond	Summoned and required to give bond.
McClannahan, William	Culpeper	Jailed for preaching.
Major, Richard	Fairfax	Warrants issued but not executed.
Major, Richard	Fauquier	Warrants issued at Bull Run—defended—Giants.
Major, Richard	Fauquier	Man went to meeting determined to kill him.

Major, Richard	Fauquier	Mob so outrageous—nearly pulled to pieces.
Marshall, Daniel	Pittsylvania	"Endured much persecution."
Marshall, William	Fauquier	Arrested but they failed to jail him.
Mash, William	Spotsylvania	Jailed for preaching. "Forty-three days."
Mastin, Thomas	Orange	Presented by grand jury.
Maxwell, Thomas	Culpeper	Jailed for preaching.
Mintz, Edward	Nansemond	Ducked and driven away in his wet clothes.
Moffett, Anderson	Culpeper	Jailed for preaching.
Moore, Jeremiah	(?)	Brutally assaulted by a mob.
Moore, Jeremiah	Fairfax	Apprehended and carried before magistrate.
Moore, Jeremiah	Fairfax	Jailed for preaching, perhaps three times.
Morton, Elijah	Orange	Ousted as a Justice because he was a Baptist.
Mullins, William	Middlesex	Presented for being absent from church.
Murphy, Joseph	(?)	Carried before magistrate, not imprisoned.
Picket, John	Fauquier	Great opposition from mobs and magistrates.
Picket, John	Culpeper	Misrepresented by Parson before congregation.
Picket, John	Culpeper	Jailed for preaching.
Picket, John	Fauquier	Jailed for preaching. Three months or more.
Pitman, Hipkins	Caroline	Arrested and threatened with whipping.
Pitman, James	Caroline	Jailed for preaching. "Sixteen days."
Pitts, Younger	Caroline	Arrested, abused, and released.
Reed, James	(?)	Dragged off stage, kicked, and cuffed about.

Reed, James	Spotsylvania	Jailed for preaching. "Forty-three days."
Saunders, Nathaniel	Culpeper	Summoned to appear at court for preaching.
Saunders, Nathaniel	Culpeper or Orange	Arrested and tried, but acquitted.
Saunders, Nathaniel	Culpeper	Jailed for preaching.
Shackelford, John	Essex	Jailed for preaching. "Eight days."
Spencer, Joseph	Orange	Jailed for preaching.
Spiller, Philip	Stafford	Jailed for preaching.
Street, Henry	Middlesex	Received one lash—prevented by companions.
Tanner, John	Chesterfield	Jailed for preaching. Gave bond.
Tanner, John	Norfleet's Ferry	Shot with a shot-gun.
Taylor, John	Hampshire	Suffered the "rage of mobs."
Thomas, David	Stafford	Violent opposition— worship prevented.
Thomas, David	Stafford	Ruffians armed with bludgeons to beat him.
Thomas, David	Culpeper or Orange	Dragged out amidst clinched fists, etc.
Thomas, David	Fauquier (?)	Pulled down while preaching—dragged out.
Thomas, David	Culpeper or Orange	Attempt made to shoot him— battle followed.
"Three Old Men"	Stafford	Indicted, fined, but not imprisoned.
Tinsley, David	Chesterfield	Jailed for preaching. Four months and 16 days.
Tribble, Andrew	Orange	Presented for preaching.
Waford, Thomas	Middlesex	Severely beaten with a whip.
Waford, Thomas	Essex	Arrested, searched, and released.
Walker, Jeremiah	James City	Opposed by the "Parson and others."

Walker, Jeremiah	Chesterfield	Jailed for preaching.
Walker, Jeremiah	Chesterfield	Denied the prison bounds.
Walker, Jeremiah	Lunenburg	Sued in two actions for baptizing two boys.
Waller, John	Hanover	Hauled about by the hair of his head.
Waller, John	(?)	Almost rent asunder by friend and foe.
Waller, John	Caroline	Jerked off stage—head beaten against ground.
Waller, John	Caroline	Whipped severely by the Sheriff.
Waller, John	Caroline	Jailed for preaching. Ten days.
Waller, John	Essex	Jailed for preaching. Fourteen days.
Waller, John	Spotsylvania	Jailed for preaching. Forty-three days.
Waller, John	Middlesex	Jailed for preaching. Forty-six days.
Ware, James	Caroline	Jailed for preaching. Sixteen days.
Ware, Robert	Middlesex	Presented for not going to church.
Ware, Robert	(?)	Annoyed by men drinking and playing cards.
Ware, Robert	Essex	Jailed for preaching. Eight days.
Ware, Robert	Middlesex	Jailed for preaching. Forty-six days.
Weatherford, John	Chesterfield	Jailed for preaching. Five months.
Weatherford, John	Chesterfield	Denied the prison bounds.
Weatherford, John	Chesterfield	Hands slashed while preaching.
Webber, William	Middlesex	Jailed for preaching. Forty-six days.
Webber, William	Chesterfield	Jailed for preaching. Three months.
Weeks, Anderson	Stafford	Arrested on a warrant, but not imprisoned.
Wyley, Allen	Orange	Jailed for preaching. "For sometime."
Young, John	Caroline	Jailed for preaching. Five or six months.

Bibliography

Alley, Reuben Edward. *A History of Baptists in Virginia*. Richmond: Virginia Baptist General Board, 1973.

Isaac, Rhys. *The Transformation of Virginia, 1740-1790*. New York & London: W. W. Norton & Co., 1982.

James, Charles F. *Documentary History of the Struggle for Religious Liberty in Virginia*. Lynchburg VA: J. P. Bell Company, 1900.

Little, Lewis Peyton. *Imprisoned Preachers and Religious Liberty in Virginia*. Lynchburg VA: J. P. Bell Co., Inc., 1938.

McIlwaine, Henry R. *The Struggle of Protestant Dissenters for Religious Toleration in Virginia*. Johns Hopkins University Press Series in Political Science. Edited by Herbert B. Adams. Baltimore: Johns Hopkins University Press, 1894.

Moore, John S. and William L. Lumpkin. *Meaningful Moments in Virginia Baptist Life, 1717-1972*. Prepared for the Sesquicentennial Celebration of the Baptist General Association of Virginia, 1973.

Peterson, Merrill D. *Thomas Jefferson & the New Nation: A Biography*. New York and London: Oxford University Press, 1970.

Ryland, Garnett. *The Baptists of Virginia, 1699-1926*. Richmond: The Virginia Baptist Board of Missions and Education, 1955.

———. *James Ireland: An Address by Garnett Ryland Delivered at the Unveiling of the Monument to James Ireland, May 20, 1931*. Richmond: The Virginia Baptist Historical Society, University of Richmond, 1931.

Semple, Robert Baylor. *History of the Baptists in Virginia*. Revised and extended by G. W. Beale, with an introduction by Dr. Joe M. King. 1894. Reprint, Gallatin TN: Church History Research and Archives, 1976.

Spencer, J. H. *A History of Kentucky Baptists*. Revised and corrected by Burrilla B. Spencer. 2 volumes. 1885. Reprint, Gallatin TN: Church History Research and Archives, 1984.

Taylor, James B. *Lives of Virginia Baptist Ministers*. Second edition, revised and enlarged. Richmond VA: Yale & Wyatt, 1838.

Taylor, John. *A History of Ten Baptist Churches of Which the Author has Alternately Been A Member*. Second edition. 1827. Reprint, New York: Arno Press, New York, 1980.

———. *Baptists on the American Frontier: A History of Ten Baptist Churches of Which the Author has Alternately Been A Member*. Edited by Chester Raymond Young. Annotated third edition. Macon GA: Mercer University Press, 1995.